Chemistry 11

THE KEY

STUDENT STUDY GUIDE

THE KEY

THE KEY series of student study guides is specifically designed to assist students in preparing for unit tests, final exams, and provincial examinations. Each ***KEY*** includes questions, answers, detailed solutions, and practice tests. The complete solutions show problem-solving methods, explain key concepts, and highlight potential errors.

TABLE OF CORRELATIONS

Castle Rock Research has designed ***THE KEY*** by correlating every question and its solution to British Columbia Ministry of Education's curriculum outcomes. Each review unit begins with a Table of Correlations that lists the General and Specific Outcomes from the British Columbia curriculum along with Related Questions that correspond to the outcomes. Usually the emphasis placed on outcomes, concepts, and skills within each unit varies. Students and teachers can quickly identify the relevant importance of each outcome and concept in the unit as determined by the number of related questions provided in ***THE KEY***.

For grades 4, 7, 10, and 12, the weighting of each unit and concept is determined by analyzing the blueprint for the respective foundation skills assessment and provincial examinations. Based on this analysis, the Related Questions for outcomes and concepts are organized on a proportionate basis. For grades other than 4, 7, 10, and 12, the breakdown of each course is determined by consulting with experienced teachers and by reviewing curriculum guides and textbooks.

The Table of Correlations is a critical component of ***THE KEY***. For students, it offers a visual cue for effectively organizing study time. For teachers, the Table of Correlations indicates the instructional focus for each content strand, serves as a curriculum checklist, and focuses on the outcomes and concepts that are the most important in the unit and the particular course of study. Students become "test wise" by becoming familiar with exam and question formats used most often in provincial examinations.

B.C. Edition

Canadian Cataloguing in Publication Data

Rao, Gautam, 1961 –
THE KEY – Chemistry 11

1. Science – Juvenile Literature. I. Title

Published by
Castle Rock Research Corp.
2340 Manulife Place
10180 – 101 Street
Edmonton, AB T5J 3S4

3 4 5 FP 05 04 03

Printed in Canada

Publisher
Gautam Rao

Editors
Mun Prasad
Shirley Wacowich

Contributors
Brian Spray

Print Production
Phil Beauchamp
Alesha Braitenbach
Tory Braybrook
Nishi Chadha
Mark Chan
Kevin Huenison
Lorraine James
Shawna Kozel
James Kropfreiter
Julie May
David Moret
Suzanne Morin
Jackie Pacheco
Tara Pratt
Abhinav Rastogi
Diana Seguin
Jan Witwicky
Gary Yaremchuk
Richard Yeomans

Castle Rock Research Corp

Dedicated to the memory of Dr. V. S. Rao

THE KEY – CHEMISTRY 11

THE KEY for Chemistry 11 is a resource that has been designed to support students in their learning, complement their classroom instruction, and help them prepare for unit tests and final exams. It is a compilation of questions, answers and detailed solutions. Questions have been grouped by concepts so students may use the resource throughout the year to study for all tests and to prepare for their final exams. The solutions help students to understand the problem-solving process in arriving at the correct response. The following is an overview of the main sections of ***THE KEY***.

I ***KEY Factors Contributing to School Success*** provides students with examples of study and review strategies. Topics include information on learning styles, study schedules, and developing review notes.

II ***Unit Review,*** with *Challenger Questions*, includes questions related to the seven chemistry units of study. All questions are classified according to the units studied in class and are correlated to the specific concept(s) being tested. In *Unit Review*, questions considered to be more difficult are labeled as *Challenger*. ***THE KEY* provides detailed solutions for all questions.**

III ***KEY Strategies for Success on Exams*** explores topics such as common exam question formats, and strategies for responding, directing words most commonly used, how to begin the exam, and managing test anxiety.

IV ***Practice Examination*** section contains a sample examination. The questions presented here are distinct from the questions in the previous section. It is recommended that students work through the exam carefully as it is reflective of the exam format and level of difficulty that students are likely to encounter on final exams. **Complete solutions are provided for all questions in this section.**

THE KEY *Study Guides* are available for English 11, Biology 11, Chemistry 11, Physics 11, and Principles of Mathematics 11. A complete list of ***THE KEY*** *Study Guides* available for grades 3 to12 appears at the end of this book and on our web site.

For information about any of our resources or services, please call Castle Rock Research at 250.868.8384 or visit our web site at http://www.castlerockresearch.com.

At Castle Rock Research we strive to produce a resource that is error-free. If you should find an error, please contact us so that future editions can be corrected.

CONTENTS

KEY Factors Contributing to School Success

Unit Review

Answers and Solutions – Unit Review

KEY Strategies for Success on Exams

Practice Examination

Answers and Solutions – Practice Examination

Appendices

KEY FACTORS CONTRIBUTING TO SCHOOL SUCCESS

School Success

KEY FACTORS CONTRIBUTING TO SCHOOL SUCCESS

You want to do well in school. There are many factors that contribute to your success. While you may not have control over the number or types of assignments and tests that you need to complete, there are many factors that you can control to improve your academic success in any subject area. The following are examples of these factors.

- **REGULAR CLASS ATTENDANCE** – helps you to master the subject content, identify key concepts, take notes and receive important handouts, ask your teacher questions, clarify information, use school resources, and meet students with whom you can study
- **POSITIVE ATTITUDE AND PERSONAL DISCIPLINE** – helps you to come to classes on time, prepared to work and learn, complete all assignments to the best of your ability, and contribute to a positive learning environment
- **SELF-MOTIVATION AND PERSONAL DISCIPLINE** – helps you to set personal learning goals, take small steps continually moving toward achieving your goals, and to "stick it out when the going gets tough"
- **ACCESSING ASSISTANCE WHEN YOU NEED IT** – helps you to improve or clarify your understanding of the concept or new learning before moving on to the next phase
- **MANAGING YOUR TIME EFFICIENTLY** – helps you to reduce anxiety and focus your study and review efforts on the most important concepts
- **DEVELOPING 'TEST WISENESS'** – helps to increase your confidence in writing exams if you are familiar with the typical exam format, common errors to avoid, and know how the concepts in a subject area are usually tested
- **KNOWING YOUR PERSONAL LEARNING STYLE** – helps you to maximize your learning by using effective study techniques, developing meaningful study notes, and make the most efficient use of your study time

KNOW YOUR LEARNING STYLE

You have a unique learning style. Knowing your learning style – how you learn best – can help you to maximize your time in class and during your exam preparation. There are seven common learning styles. Read the following descriptions to see which one most closely describes your learning preferences.

- **LINGUISTIC LEARNER** (sometimes referred to as an auditory learner) – learns best by saying, hearing and seeing words; is good at memorizing things such as dates, places, names and facts
- **LOGICAL/MATHEMATICAL LEARNER** – learns best by categorizing, classifying and working with abstract relationships; is good at mathematics, problem solving and reasoning
- **SPATIAL LEARNER** (sometimes referred to as a visual learner) – learns best by visualizing, seeing, working with pictures; is good at puzzles, imaging things, and reading maps and charts
- **MUSICAL LEARNER** – learns best by hearing, rhythm, melody, and music; is good at remembering tones, rhythms and melodies, picking up sounds
- **BODILY/KINESTHETIC LEARNER** – learns best by touching, moving, and processing knowledge through bodily sensations; is good at physical activities
- **INTERPERSONAL LEARNER** – learns best by sharing, comparing, relating, cooperating; is good at organizing, communicating, leading, and understanding others
- **INTRAPERSONAL LEARNER** – learns best by working alone, individualized projects, and self-paced instruction

(Adapted from http://snow.utoronto.ca/Learn2/mod3/mistyles.html)

Your learning style may not fit "cleanly" into one specific category but may be a combination of two or more styles. Knowing your personal learning style allows you to organize your study notes in a manner that provides you with the most meaning. For example, if you are a spatial or visual learner, you may find mind mapping and webbing are effective ways to organize subject concepts, information, and study notes. If you are a linguistic learner, you may need to write and then "say out loud" the steps in a process, the formula, or actions that lead up to a significant event. If you are a kinesthetic learner you may need to use your finger to trace over a diagram to remember it or to "tap out" the steps in solving a problem or "feel" yourself writing or typing the formula.

SCHEDULING STUDY TIME

Effective time management skills are an essential component to your academic success. The more effectively you manage your time the more likely you are to achieve your goals such as completing all of your assignments on time or finishing all of the questions on a unit test or year-end exam. Developing a study schedule helps to ensure you have adequate time to review the subject content and prepare for the exam.

You should review your class notes regularly to ensure you have a clear understanding of the new material. Reviewing your lessons on a regular basis helps you to learn and remember the ideas and concepts. It also reduces the quantity of material that you must study prior to a unit test or year-end exam. If this practice is not part of your study habits, establishing a study schedule will help you to make the best use of your time. The following are brief descriptions of three types of study schedules.

- **LONG-TERM STUDY SCHEDULE** – begins early in the school year or semester and well in advance of an exam; is the **most effective** manner for improving your understanding and retention of the concepts, and increasing self-confidence; involves regular, nightly review of class notes, handouts and text material
- **SHORT-TERM STUDY SCHEDULE** – begins **five to seven days prior to an exam**; must organize the volume of material to be covered beginning with the most difficult concepts; each study session starts with a brief review of what was studied the day before
- **CRAMMING** – occurs the night before an exam; is the **least effective** form of studying or exam preparation; focuses on memorizing and reviewing critical information such as facts, dates, formulas; do not introduce new material; has the potential to increase exam anxiety by discovering something you do not know

Regardless of the type of study schedule you use, you may want to consider the following to maximize your study time and effort:

- establish a regular time and place for doing your studying
- minimize distractions and interruptions during your study time
- plan a ten minute break for every hour that you study
- organize the material so you begin with the most challenging content first

- divide the subject content into smaller manageable "chunks" to review
- develop a marking system for your study notes to identify key and secondary concepts, concepts that you are confident about, those that require additional attention or about which you have questions
- reward yourself for sticking to your schedule and/or completing each review section
- alternate the subjects and type of study activities to maintain your interest and motivation
- make a daily task list with the headings "must do", "should do", and "could do"
- begin each session by quickly reviewing what you studied the day before
- maintain your usual routine of eating, sleeping, and exercising to help you concentrate for extended periods of time

KEY STRATEGIES FOR REVIEWING

Reviewing textbook material, class notes, and handouts should be an ongoing activity and becomes more critical in preparing for exams. You may find some of the following strategies useful in completing your review during your scheduled study time.

READING OR SKIMMING FOR KEY INFORMATION

- Before reading the chapter, preview it by noting headings, charts and graphs, chapter questions.
- Turn each heading and sub-heading into a question before you start to read.
- Read the complete introduction to identify the key information that is addressed in the chapter.
- Read the first sentence of the next paragraph for the main idea.
- Skim the paragraph noting key words, phrases, and information.
- Read the last sentence of the paragraph.
- Repeat the process for each paragraph and section until you have skimmed the entire chapter.
- Read the complete conclusion to summarize each chapter's contents.
- Answer the questions you created.
- Answer the chapter questions.

CREATING STUDY NOTES

Mind Mapping or Webbing

- Use the key words, ideas or concepts from your reading or class notes to create a *mind map or web* (a diagram or visual representation of the information). A mind map or web is sometimes referred to as a knowledge map.
- Write the key word, concept, theory or formula in the centre of your page.
- Write and link related facts, ideas, events, and information to the central concept using lines.
- Use coloured markers, underlining, or other symbols to emphasize things such as relationships, information of primary and secondary importance.
- The following example of a mind map or web illustrates how this technique can be used to develop an essay.

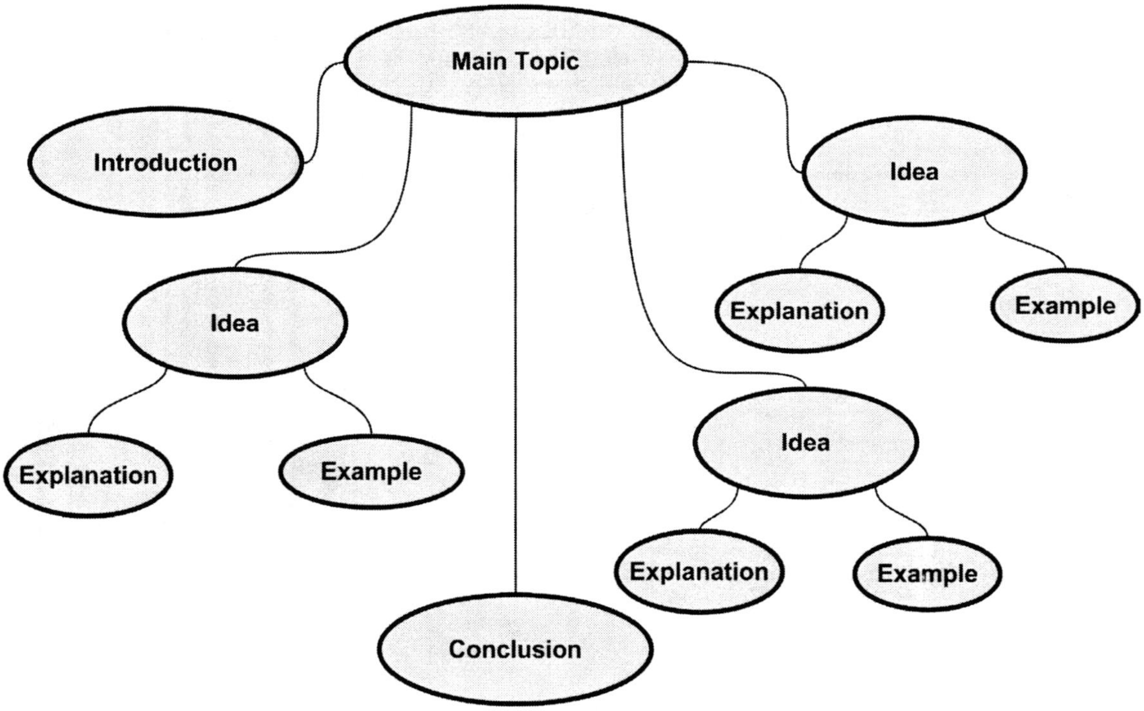

Charts

- Use charts to organize your information and relate theories, concepts, definitions, applications and other important details.
- Collect and enter the information in key categories.
- Use the completed chart as a composite picture of the concept or information.

The following is an example of how a chart can be used to help you organize information when exploring an issue in subjects such as Social Studies, the Sciences, or Humanities.

<table>
<tr><th colspan="6">Define Key Words</th></tr>
<tr><td colspan="6">1.</td></tr>
<tr><td colspan="6">2.</td></tr>
<tr><td colspan="6">3.</td></tr>
<tr><th colspan="6">Explore the Issue</th></tr>
<tr><th colspan="2">Yes to the Issue</th><th colspan="2">No to the Issue</th><th colspan="2">Maybe to the Issue</th></tr>
<tr><td colspan="2">1.</td><td colspan="2">1.</td><td colspan="2">1.</td></tr>
<tr><td colspan="2">2.</td><td colspan="2">2.</td><td colspan="2">2.</td></tr>
<tr><td colspan="2">3.</td><td colspan="2">3.</td><td colspan="2">3.</td></tr>
<tr><th colspan="6">Case Studies and Examples</th></tr>
<tr><td colspan="3">1.</td><td colspan="3">1.</td></tr>
<tr><td colspan="3">2.</td><td colspan="3">2.</td></tr>
<tr><td colspan="3">3.</td><td colspan="3">3.</td></tr>
<tr><th colspan="6">Defence of Your Point of View</th></tr>
<tr><td colspan="6">1.</td></tr>
<tr><td colspan="6">2.</td></tr>
<tr><td colspan="6">3.</td></tr>
</table>

Index Cards

- Write a key event, fact, concept, theory, word or question on one side of the index card.
- On the reverse side, write the date, place, important actions and key individuals involved in the event, significance of the fact, salient features of the concept, essence and application of the theory, definition of the word or answer to the question.
- Use the cards to quickly review important information.

International System of Units (SI)

International System of Units (SI)

SI base unit

Base quantity	Name	Symbol
length	metre	m
mass	kilogram	kg
time	second	s
amount of substance	mole	mol

Derived Measures

Measures	Unit	Symbol
Volume	cubic metre	m^3

SI Prefixes

Factor	Name	Symbol
10^6	mega	*M*
10^3	kilo	*k*
10^{-2}	centi	*c*
10^{-3}	milli	*m*
10^{-6}	micro	*μ*

Symbols

- Develop your own symbols to use when reviewing your material to identify information you need in preparing for your exam. For example, an exclamation mark (!) may signify something that "must be learned well" because it is a key concept that is likely to appear on unit tests and the year-end exam. A question mark (?) may identify something you are unsure of while a star or asterisk (*) may identify important information for formulating an argument. A check mark (✓) or an (×) can be used to show that you agree or disagree with the statement, sentence or paragraph.

Crib Notes

- Develop brief notes that are a critical summary of the essential concepts, dates, events, theories, formulas, supporting facts, or steps in a process that are most likely to be on the exam.
- Use your crib notes as your "last minute" review before you go in to write your exam. You can not take crib notes into an exam.

MEMORIZING

- **ASSOCIATION** relates the new learning to something you already know. For example, in distinguishing between the spelling of 'dessert' and 'desert', you know 'sand' has only one 's' and so should desert.
- **MNEMONIC DEVICES** are sentences you create to remember a list or group of items. For example, the first letters of the words in the sentence "**E**very **G**ood **B**oy **D**eserves **F**udge" helps you to remember the names of the lines on the treble clef staff (E, G, B, D, and F) in music.
- **ACRONYMS** are words formed from the first letters of the words in a group. For example, **HOMES** helps you to remember the names of Canada's five Great Lakes (**H**uron, **O**ntario, **M**ichigan, **E**rie, and **S**uperior).
- **VISUALIZING** requires you to use your mind's eye to "see" the chart, list, map, diagram, or sentence as it exists in your textbook, notes, on the board, computer screen or in the display.

NOTES

Introduction to Chemistry

INTRODUCTION TO CHEMISTRY

Table of Correlations		
Outcomes		**Questions**
Students are expected to:		
Lab Safety	1.1.1 list the safety and protective equipment available in the laboratory	
	1.1.2 describe how and when to use each piece of equipment	
	1.1.3 indicate on a school map the location of the nearest fire alarm and appropriate fire exits	
	1.1.4 list sources of first-aid assistance other than the classroom teacher	
	1.1.5 describe common chemistry laboratory hazards	1
	1.1.6 describe the appropriate procedure or technique for dealing with particular hazards	2,3,4
	1.1.7 produce a list of general rules of safe laboratory conduct	
	1.1.8 display a conscious safety attitude in the laboratory	
Measurement and Communication	1.2.1 use SI units and their accepted alternatives in chemistry	5,6,7,8,9,10
	1.2.2 demonstrate skills in measuring mass, volume (liquid), and temperature	WR1, WR2
	1.2.3 describe the imprecise nature of all measurements	
	1.2.4 determine the number of significant figures in a measured quantity and relate to the uncertainty	11 WR3
	1.2.5 round off calculated results to the appropriate number of significant figures	WR4
	1.2.6 correctly determine the unit of a derived quantity	
	1.2.7 state the acceptability of the numerical results of a lab experiment with regard to the uncertainty of the results	
	1.2.8 communicate results and data in clear and understandable forms	
Matter and Its Changes	1.3.1 define matter	
	1.3.2 describe chemistry as the science concerned with the properties, composition, and behaviour of matter	12, 13
	1.3.3 describe and give examples of a variety of forms and properties that matter can exhibit	
	1.3.4 distinguish between observation and interpretation	
	1.3.5 describe the types of changes that may be observed when matter is heated, combined, or separated	
	1.3.6 differentiate between physical and chemical changes	
	1.3.7 classify a substance as solid, liquid, or gas, and describe its different properties	
	1.3.8 define boiling point, freezing point, and melting point	
	1.3.9 describe the simple molecular motions and arrangements for solids, liquids, and gases	
	1.3.10 relate the heat changes that occur during phase changes to changes in molecular motions and arrangements	14, 15

INTRODUCTION TO CHEMISTRY

LAB SAFETY

1.1.1 List the safety and protective equipment in the laboratory

1.1.2 Describe how and when to use each piece of equipment

1.1.3 Indicate on a school map the location of the nearest fire alarm and appropriate fire exits

1.1.4 List sources of first-aid assistance other than the classroom teacher

It is important to be familiar with the placement and use of safety equipment in any chemistry laboratory. Your teacher will usually give specific safety precautions to be aware of before every lab. The best safety device is your brain – do not fool around in a lab and think about what you will do before acting. In the event of an accident it is important to inform the teacher but also do not hesitate to use the appropriate safety equipment.

Safety Equipment

a) Safety glasses

Safety goggles or safety glasses should be worn at all times in a chemistry laboratory when any work with chemicals is being done. The goggles are superior to glasses as they afford better eye protection from any splashes that may occur. They should be worn until all chemicals in the laboratory have been put away.

If you are wearing contacts in a chemistry lab it is best to inform the teacher. Be sure to wash your hands before touching anywhere near your eyes after being in the lab. Any chemicals that may get into your eyes could get behind the contacts. It is not recommended to wear contacts in any chemistry laboratory.

b) Fire extinguishers

Make sure you are aware of the locations of all the fire extinguishers in the room. There are usually more than one. Pay careful attention when the teacher explains the use of the fire extinguishers. If you forget or are unsure of proper use ask the teacher for clarification. A general rule of thumb is that large extinguishers will last for 20-25 seconds when used and small extinguishers will last for 10-15 seconds when used. They are good for small fires only and should it appear that a fire extinguisher is inadequate then evacuate the building and make sure to pull the fire alarm on the way out. Do not use a fire extinguisher on a person especially near their head as it is possible to blind them.

c) Fire blanket

Make sure you are aware of the location of the fire blanket in the classroom. It is possible to use the fire blanket when a student's clothing catches fire. It is a much better practice to stop, drop and roll if your clothing catches fire. The fire blanket can also be used to smother a small fire in the classroom.

If there is a fire, inform the teacher and other students immediately. Do not be shy about this. If the fire is small and contained, such as in a beaker, it may be possible to smother it with other glass ware. Cover the top of the beaker with another beaker or watch glass. A lab coat or the fire blanket can also be used to smother a small fire. If the fire is small and uncontained you or the teacher could use a fire extinguisher to put it out. If the fire is not small and appears too large for a fire extinguisher then pull the fire alarm and evacuate the building.

d) Emergency shower

The emergency shower is used when some form of hazardous chemical is spilled on the body. Typically these spills are of corrosive or caustic chemicals such as acids or bases. It is necessary for the student to remain in the shower for long enough to thoroughly rinse the affected area. Let the teacher or the first aid attendant be the judge of how long to remain in the shower. Affected clothing needs to be removed while in the shower and replaced.

e) Eye wash fountain

The eye wash fountain is to be used whenever there is a spill or splash of any chemical that contacts the eyes. It is important that everyone is aware of the eye wash location and is prepared to lead the splash victim to it and help use it. Try to keep the eyes open as much as possible when flushing with the water to allow for maximum rinsing. The minimum time to flush the eyes is 15 minutes but let the teacher or first aid attendant be the one to say exactly how long. Do not take any chances with your vision.

f) Acid/base neutralizing solution

This is not a safety device but is necessary in a chemistry laboratory. Its purpose is to buffer an acid or base spill and make it safer to clean up the chemicals. This solution is for use on spills that are not on a person. Do not use the acid/base neutralizing solution on a person. A spill on any individual should be flushed with running water in a sink, the eye wash station or in the emergency shower, depending upon the location and size of the spill.

1.1.5 Describe common chemistry laboratory hazards

1.1.6 Describe appropriate procedures or techniques for dealing with particular hazards

1.1.7 Produce a list of general rules of safe laboratory conduct

1.1.8 Display a conscious safety attitude in the laboratory

a) Broken glass

Freshly broken glass is amongst the sharpest substances on earth. Do not pick up broken glass with your hands. Inform the teacher of the accident and if you are instructed to clean up then use a dust pan and broom. Ask your teacher for specific directions if there are chemicals mixed in with the glass.

Never use any lab glassware that is cracked or is chipped. It could easily break if heated or bumped and spill chemicals and/or cause a cut. Dispose this sort of glassware in the broken glass container usually present in any lab.

b) Bunsen burners

Do not leave gas on for more than 4-5 seconds while trying to light the Bunsen burner. If you are unable to light if then ask for assistance from the teacher. Be careful to keep combustible materials such as paper or flammable liquids away form the Bunsen burner while lighting and operating it.

When heating a substance in a test tube with a Bunsen burner ensure that the test tube is at a slight angle and is pointing away from you and anyone else nearby. This will avoid any chance that the substance will contact anyone should it over heat and splash or spit out. Never heat any substance in a sealed container as the vapour pressure will increase and could cause the container to shatter or the top to blow off and chemicals to shoot out. Lastly, when heating glass with a Bunsen burner or even a hot plate, just remember that hot glass looks like cold glass; do not touch the glass to see if it is too hot. Use the back of your hand near the glass to feel for heat, it is more sensitive than the bottom of your hand.

c) Spilled chemicals

Be aware of any chemical outside of a labelled container. Keep in mind that many solutions may look like water but contain toxic or corrosive substances. Inform the teacher of any spill and if you are to clean it up follow the specific directions you receive. Assume all chemicals outside of a container are hazardous and treat them as such. Should any of the spilled chemical get on your hands, rinse thoroughly under running water for several minutes or until instructed to stop by your teacher or a first aid attendant. Clothing with spilled chemicals on them should be removed as soon as possible and washed. If the spill contacts the eye or near the eye use the eyewash fountain immediately. If it is a large spill on the body use the emergency shower, to thoroughly flush the area affected and remove clothes that are affected.

d) Safety tip

Think before you act in a chemistry lab and you will likely avoid all accidents. Avoid loose clothing, dangling strings or jewellery and tie back long hair to avoid knocking over chemicals, getting the hair or dangling article in the chemicals or lighting any of it on fire with a Bunsen burner.

e) Disposal of chemicals

The teacher will likely give you instructions for disposal of all chemicals before any lab. If you are unsure of what the instructions were then ask your teacher for clarification. Many substances are toxic to the environment and will not be disposed of down the sink. A general rule of thumb is that unused chemicals never go back in their original container.

Related Questions: 1–4

MEASUREMENT AND COMMUNICATION

1.2.1 Use SI units and their values in Chemistry

1.2.2 Demonstrate skills in measuring mass, volume (liquid), and temperature

SI, International System, of metric units is the standard form of measurement in science. The common units used in Chemistry 11 are summarized in the following table:

UNIT	SYMBOL	MEASURES
Metre	m	Length
Kilogram	kg	Mass
Second	s	Time
Mole	mol	Amount of a substance
Derived Measures		
Metre	m^3	Volume

SI Prefixes		
NAME	SYMBOL	FACTOR
Micro	μ	10^{-6}
Milli	m	10^{-3}
Centi	c	10^{-2}
Kilo	k	10^{3}
Mega	M	10^{6}

Related Questions: 6-11, WR1-WR4

1.2.3 Describe the imprecise nature of all measurements

1.2.4 Determine the number of significant figures in a measured quantity and relate to the uncertainty

1.2.5 Round off calculated results to the appropriate number of significant figures

The numbers we work with in chemistry, or any science, are only as good as the tools we use to acquire them. The calculations we do with these values must reflect the accuracy of our instruments. Values which we know are very clearly measured are known as certain digits. The certain digits are followed by an uncertain digit which is an estimate and is just outside the ability of the instrument to measure precisely. The combination of the certain digits and the one uncertain digit are known as the significant figures.

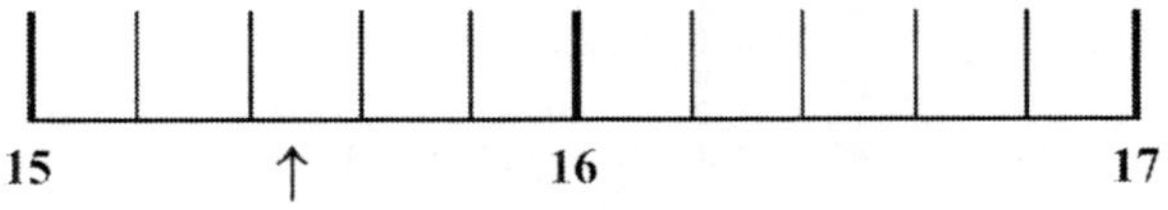

Refer to the example ruler above. The arrow is indicating a point which is clearly between 15 and 16 so we are certain the value is at least 15. Each small division between 15 and 16 has a value of 0.2 so we can further state that the arrow is indicating a point between 15.4 and 15.6 so we are certain the value is at least 15.4. We could further guess the indicated point is at 15.46 but the last digit, the 6, is somewhat uncertain as it is an estimate. The 6 has some significance but not as much as the 15.4 and is thus referred to as the uncertain digit. This measurement, 15.46, has four significant figures; three certain digits and one uncertain digit.

Significant digits and when zero is significant

- all nonzero digits are significant
- zeroes are significant if they appear between nonzero digits. e.g. 101
- zeroes are significant if they appear to the right of a nonzero digit and there is a decimal place present. e.g. 20.0

Examples

- **15** has two significant figures
- 10 has one significant figure as the zero does not count
- **101** has three significant figures as the zero counts because it is between two nonzero digits
- **10.0** has three significant figures as the zeroes are to the right of the nonzero digit and there is a decimal place
- 0.0**50** has two significant figures; the first two zeroes are not significant and are merely place values; the last zero is significant as it is to the right of a nonzero digit and there is a decimal place
- **1.30** $\times 10^{-4}$ has three significant figures; all numbers are significant in scientific notation

Operations with significant figures

- Any number that represents a numerical count or is an exact definition has an unlimited number of significant figures and is considered to be an absolute value.
- Superfluous digits, those beyond the significant figures, are rounded to the nearest significant figure. If it is 5 or more it is rounded up and if it is less than five the superfluous digit is dropped.
- In multiplication and division the answer of the operation can have no more significant figures than the factor having the fewest number of significant figures.
- The root or power of a number will have as many significant figures as the number.
- When adding or subtracting arrange the numbers in columns and round any numbers to the right of the least certain digit present.

Examples

- $45.0 \div 9.0 = 5.0$ The answer, 5.0, can have two significant figures as 9.0 has two significant figures, and the answer can only be as accurate as the least accurate value used in any multiplication or division operation.
- $46.4 + 4 + 100.55 = 151$ The 4 is the least certain of the numbers given as it is only giving a value to the ones position, while the 46.4 is giving values to the tenths position and 100.55 is giving values to the hundredths position. All digits must then be rounded to the ones position to reflect the accuracy of the 4. The answer can be no more accurate the least accurate value used.

Related Question: 11

1.2.6 Correctly determine the units of a derived quantity

Derived Units

These are units that are produced by combining two or more other units. A common use of this in everyday life is velocity; *Km*/*hr*. Velocity is the combination of distance and time.

Velocity = distance per time

$v = m/s$ as a base unit and is converted to *Km*/*hr* when used as a speed in our society. Velocity's unit is *m*/*s* or *Km*/*hr* which are derived units combining the units of distance and time.

Density is a common derived unit used in chemistry and is a function of mass and volume.

Density = mass/volume
$d = g/mL$ or g/cm^3

1.2.7 State the acceptability of the numerical results of a lab experiment with regard to the uncertainty of the results

1.2.8 Communicate results and data in clear and understandable forms

Experimental uncertainty refers to the degree to which any measured value might be in error. The uncertainty for any measurement is indicated after the number.

Example

35.6 ± 0.1 mm this tells us that the value lies between 35.5mm and 35.7mm

MATTER AND ITS CHANGES

1.3.1 Define matter

1.3.2 Describe chemistry as the science concerned with the properties, composition and behaviour of matter

1.3.3 Describe and give examples of a variety of forms and properties that matter can exhibit

1.3.4 Distinguish between observation and interpretation

1.3.5 Describe the types of changes that may be observed when matter is heated, combined, or separated

1.3.6 Differentiate between physical and chemical changes

1.3.7 Classify a substance as solid, liquid, or gas, and describe its different properties

1.3.8 Define boiling point, freezing point, and melting point

1.3.9 Describe the simple molecular motions and arrangements for solids, liquids, and gases

1.3.10 Relate the heat changes that occur during phase changes to changes in molecular motions and arrangements

Matter can be defined as anything that has mass and occupies space. There are more issues with this simple definition than one would first think. For example why does matter exist? Mass can be defined as an object's resistance to a change in its motion but this explains little as to what or why matter really is. Space then also becomes difficult to describe; its definition is fairly circular – space is that which is occupied by matter yet space is used in the definition of matter.

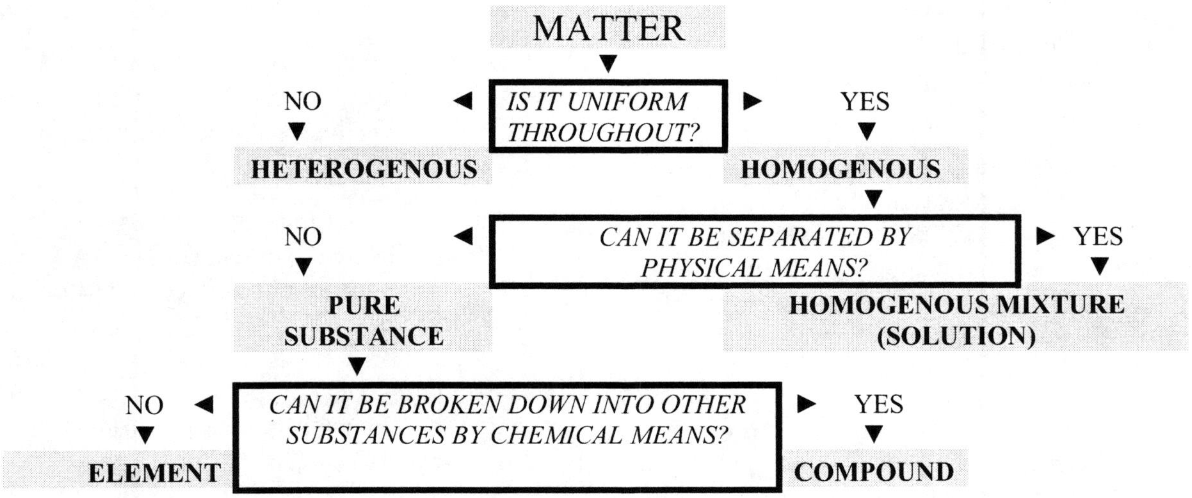

a) Elements

These are pure substances which cannot be broken down by further chemical means. An atom can be destroyed but not by chemical means; it requires a nuclear reaction. An element is composed of only one kind of atom.

b) Compounds

These are pure substances composed of two or more atoms of different elements chemically bonded together. A compound can be destroyed by chemical means. It can be broken down into the elements it is composed of or it can be combined with other elements or compounds to produce new substances.

c) Mixtures

These pure substances are composed of two or more substances, but each keeps its original properties.

d) Atom

It is the smallest object that retains properties of an element. It is composed of electrons and a nucleus (containing protons and neutrons).

e) Molecule

These pure substances are simply two or more atoms chemically bonded together. The atoms do not have to be different atoms and a molecule can be broken down by chemical means into the atoms of which it is made.

Chemistry is the science that is concerned with the properties, composition and behaviour of matter. All substances have a unique set of properties which will characterize their behaviour. These properties can also be used to identify the substances. There are two types of properties used in chemistry:

- Physical properties: these are properties that can be established without changing the actual substance. Some examples of physical properties are density, colour, electrical conductivity, thermal conductivity, melting and boiling points and hardness.
- Chemical properties: these properties describe the substance's ability to chemically react and produce new substances with new properties. Some examples of chemical properties would be iron's ability to react to oxidize in the presence of oxygen and water to produce Iron III oxide (rust) and hydrogen's ability to violently burn with oxygen to produce water.

Physical Change involves changes that are observable but do not change the underlying structure of the substance. Such change includes freezing, evaporating, or filtering.

Chemical Change occurs when chemical reactions create new chemical substances. Evidence that chemical change has occurred may be energy (heat) release, formation of a gas or precipitate, a colour change, or an odour change.

All substances will exist in one of the various states (phases) of matter. There are several phases of matter but only three which are relevant at this time – solid, liquid and gas.

- Solid: definite shape, definite volume
- Liquid: indefinite shape, definite volume
- Gas: indefinite shape, indefinite volume

Indefinite shape means the substance does not take on the shape of the container. Indefinite volume means the substance would expand to fill the entire compound.

These are the common states of matter used in chemistry. There are other states of matter such as plasma and Bose-Einstein condensate, but they are commonly thought of as in the realm of physics. Plasma exists at extremely high temperatures, several million degrees Celsius, and exists as nuclei and free electrons. Bose-Einstein condensate exists at extremely low temperatures near absolute zero where many atoms of an element are thought to merge into one super atom of the element.

No matter what state matter is in it will be in motion unless the temperature is absolute zero (-273°C). Anything in motion has kinetic energy and there are three basic ways, thus energies, in which molecules can be moving.

- Translational energy – the molecule is moving in a straight line
- Rotational energy – the molecule is rotating about one of its axes
- Vibrational energy – the molecule is vibrating and the bond lengths and angles between atoms are changing

Energy and phase changes

Matter in the solid state has the least amount of energy and the molecules are not moving about freely but are vibrating. As the kinetic energy of the matter increases, usually due to a temperature increase, the molecules begin to oscillate back and forth. The energy gained is mostly translational and vibrational energy. They will impact their neighbours more frequently and with greater force as the kinetic energy increases. At a given point for any type of matter the molecules will have enough energy to break the bonds which hold them as a solid and move apart from one another. This is melting and the matter is in the liquid state with the molecules moving about freely.

The molecules in the liquid state will also move about with greater speed as energy is continually added to the system. They will move about with ever increasing speed until they have enough energy to break away from the other molecules. This is boiling and the matter is in the gas phase.

Substances will go through phase changes as temperature changes. The heating curve below shows the typical behaviour of a pure substance as it is heated.

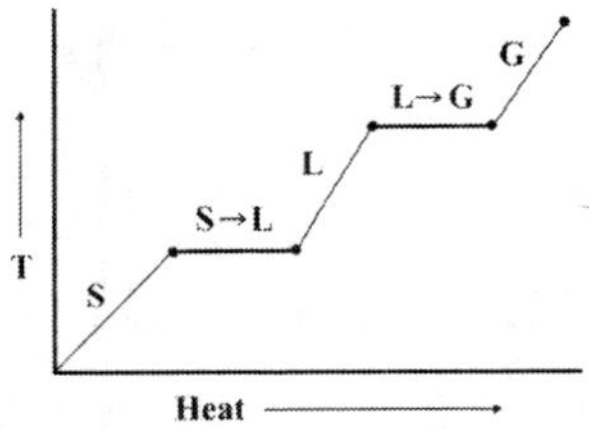

On the above graph the temperature of the solid, (S), increases until it hits the melting point. The melting temperature and the freezing temperature of a pure substance are the same, depending upon whether or not the temperature is increasing or decreasing. At the melting point, the graph plateaus as all the energy entering the system is being used to change phase from solid to liquid (L). Solid and liquid will coexist at this temperature. Once the solid has changed phase into liquid the temperature will again increase until the liquid hits the boiling point of the substance. At this temperature the substance begins to change phase into a gas (G) and the temperature plateaus. All the heat entering the system is being used to for the state change. Liquid and gas will coexist at this temperature. Once the liquid has changed phase into a gas the temperature will again begin to rise.

Related Questions: 12-15

1. A clear unlabelled beaker with a small crack containing what looks like water is sitting on a lab bench beside a lit Bunsen burner. What are the hazards that are **most likely** present in this situation?

A. The unknown solution may be hazardous, the beaker may break if moved, and the glass may be hot.

B. The water in glass may be hot, and it is possible the glass could break if dropped on floor.

C. The solution may be dangerous and may leak out of the crack if the solution is heated.

D. The solution is not labelled and may be dangerous, and the heat from the burner may break the glass.

PARTNERS IN EDUCATION

Use the following information to answer the next question.

Wearing a seatbelt significantly reduces your chance of serious injury or death in a crash. A young driver who always wears a seatbelt and obeys the rules of the road is compared to a chemistry student who follows safety precautions and wears the necessary protective equipment in a science laboratory.

2. Which of the following statements does not describe how the driver and the student are similar?

A. Both display a conscious safety attitude.
B. Neither will be involved in an accident.
C. Both are responsible not only to themselves but also to the people around them.
D. By taking preventative measures, each has reduced the potential for accident or injury.

ICBC Road Sense

3. If a small fire starts in the classroom you should immediately

A. use the fire extinguisher and inform the teacher and class of the fire
B. tell the teacher and ask for permission to use the fire extinguisher
C. run from the room, pull the fire alarm and then go tell the teacher
D. yell out a warning to the class and then run out to pull fire alarm

4. What should you do if your lab partner catches her hair and shirt on fire in the Bunsen burner?

A. Have her run to an emergency shower to douse the flames.
B. Have her stop, drop, and roll, and then help her smother the flames.
C. Have her move quickly to the fire blanket and smother the flames.
D. Have her shove her head under the tap and splash water on the shirt.

5. The metric base unit for measuring distance is

A. acre **B.** celsius
C. kilometre **D.** metre

6. Which of the following is **not** an SI base unit?

A. Metre **B.** Second
C. Centigrade **D.** Millilitre

7. How many millimetres are in 2.5 kilometres?

A. 2.5×10^{-6} mm
B. 2.5×10^{-3} mm
C. 2.5×10^{3} mm
D. 2.5×10^{6} mm

8. To accurately convert 7.62 mm to m in one step, you should

A. multiply 7.62 mm by 1000
B. divide 7.62 mm by 1000
C. move the decimal in 7.62 two places to the left
D. move the decimal in 7.62 two places to the right

9. Convert 1.750×10^{5} L to mL.

A. 1.75×10^{9} mL
B. 175,000 mL
C. 1.750×10^{2} mL
D. 1.750×10^{8} mL

10. Convert 13.5 kg into micrograms.

A. 1.35×10^{10} μg **B.** 1.35×10^{7} μg
C. 1.35×10^{-8} $\mu g3$ **D.** 1.35×10^{4} μg

11. Which of the following does not have three significant figures?

A. 1 340 **B.** 0.078

C. 1.55×10^{-2} **D.** 0.0105

Use the following information to answer the next question.

I	Air
II	Methane
III	Water
IV	Silver
V	Carbon dioxide

12. Which of the following statements is correct?

A. I, III and IV are elements.
B. II, III and V are compounds.
C. III and IV are elements.
D. III and IV are mixtures.

Use the following list to answer the next question.

I	Zinc
II	Hydrogen
III	Brass
IV	Silver
V	Soap solution

13. Which of the following statements is correct?

A. I, III and IV are elements.
B. II, III and V are mixtures.
C. I, II and IV are elements.
D. III and IV are compounds.

14. What is the effect on the particles in a system if heat is added to the system?

A. They begin to move faster and the temperature decreases.
B. They begin to move faster and the temperature increases.
C. They begin to move slower and the temperature increases.
D. They begin to move slower and the temperature decreases.

15. As translation energy of a system is reduced, the volume of the system

A. decreases
B. increases
C. doubles
D. remains constant

Written Response

1. A pure gold nugget has a mass of 3.56 g and volume of 0.184 cm^3. What is the density of the gold nugget?

2. A 4.5g piece of iron is dropped into a graduated cylinder containing 10.2mL of water. Given that the density of iron is 7.9 g/cm^3, what is the new volume reading on the graduated cylinder?

3. Determine the number of significant figures for each of the following:

i) 120
ii) 1.050
iii) 0.345
iv) 1010
v) 6.02×10^{23}

4. Calculate the following showing the answer using correct significant figures.

i) $237050 \times 3.41 =$
ii) $435.00 \div 0.03100 =$
iii) $23.1 + 2.55 + 9.367 =$

NOTES

Atoms, Molecules, and Ions

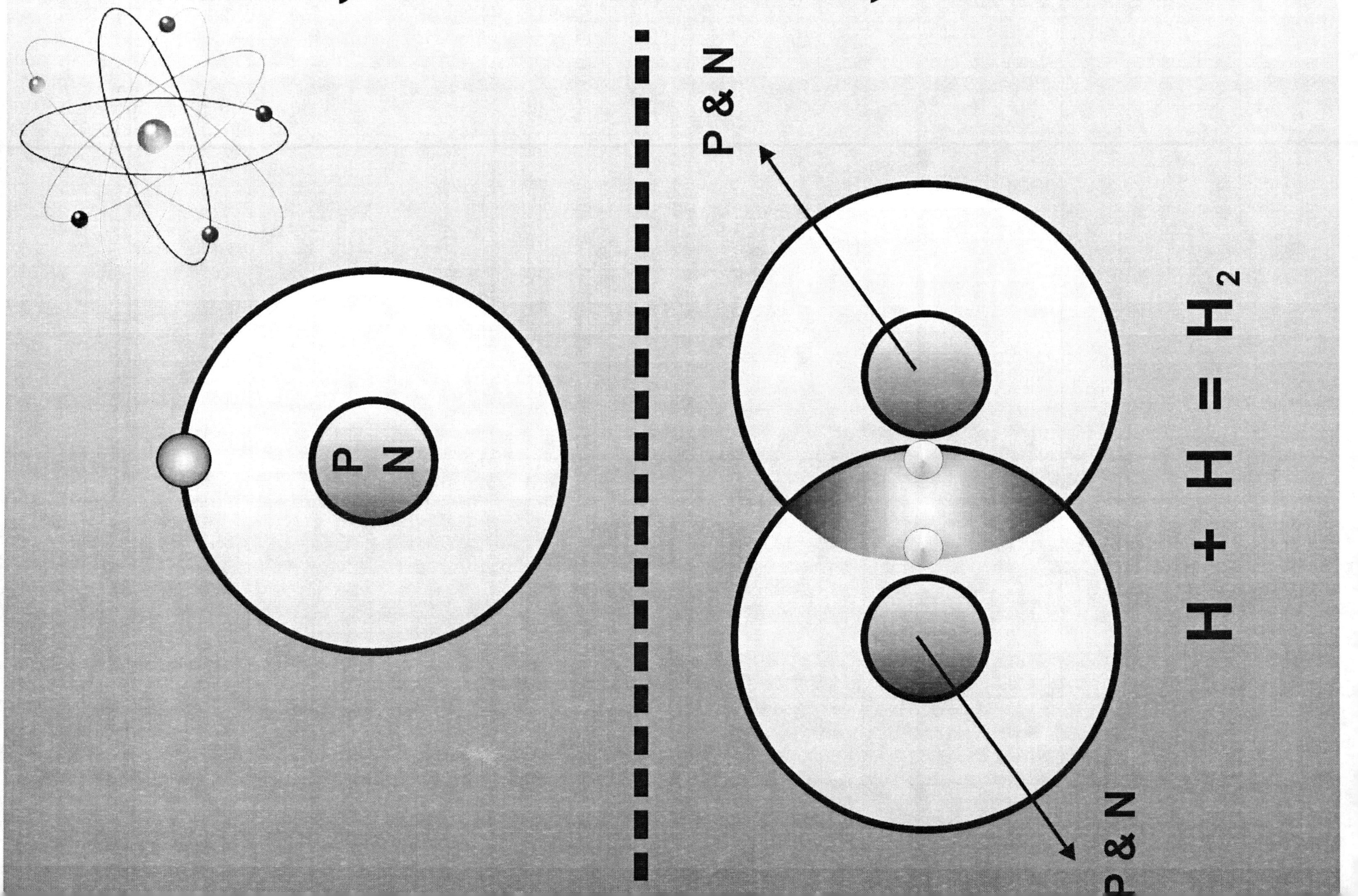

ATOMS, MOLECULES, AND IONS

Table of Correlations		
Outcomes		**Questions**
Students are expected to:		
Classification	2.1.1 describe a substance as having a set of unique and identifiable properties	
	2.1.2 classify a given material as an element, compound, or mixture, using the properties of the material	
	2.1.3 describe several ways that substances may be separated from one another	2
	2.1.4 relate the observable properties and characteristics of elements, compounds, and mixtures to the concept of atoms and molecules	
	2.1.5 define atom, molecule, and ion	1
Nomenclature	2.2.1 write chemical symbols for elements and formulae for ions from appropriate charts	3, 13
	2.2.2 name the ionic compound from a formula, and write the formula given a name	4, 5
	2.2.3 name the covalent compound from a formula using the prefix naming system, and write the formula given a name	6, 7, 8, 9, 10, 11, WR1
	2.2.4 predict the formulae of covalent compounds given the formula of another compound containing elements in the same family (families)	12
	2.2.5 write the names and formulae for some common acids	14

ATOMS, MOLECULES, AND IONS

CLASSIFICATION

2.1.1 Describe a substance as having a set of unique and identifiable properties

Any substance has a set of properties which are collectively unique to it and are uniform throughout it. These properties can be used to identify the substance. Examples of these properties are density, boiling temperature, melting temperature, hardness, malleability, lustre and ductility. Not all properties would be used for all substances however determining several of them would allow you to classify the substance in question.

2.1.2 Classify a given material as an element or mixture using the properties of the material

The following classification of matter is based upon its initial appearance and then by whether it can be separated by physical or chemical means:

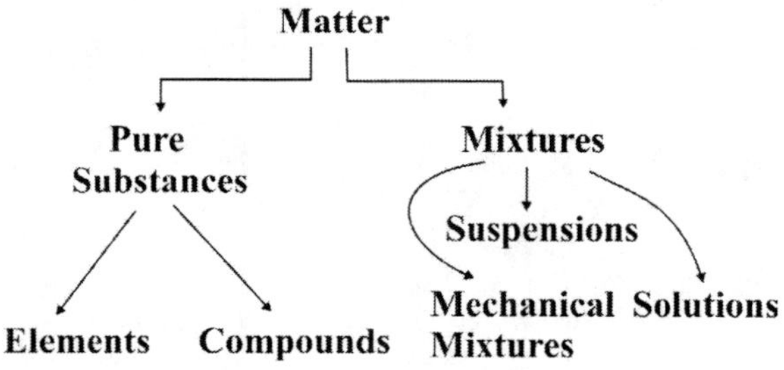

2.1.3 Describe several ways that substances can be separated from one another

a) Hand Separation

This is the actual act of picking apart a mixture using your hands or perhaps a sieve or magnet. This method is only possible with mechanical mixtures.

b) Filtration

This method is good for separating a solid from a liquid as long as the solid is not in solution with the liquid. It is in essence a mechanical mixture.

c) Evaporation

This method is again good for separating a solid from a liquid. It allows you to retain the solid after the liquid has evaporated away. It can be done with mechanical mixtures of solid and liquid and with solids that are in solution with the liquid. Evaporation will not allow you to retain the liquid as it is lost to the atmosphere.

d) Distillation

This method is primarily for mixtures of liquids where the liquids are in solution with one another. The liquids will have different boiling temperatures as they are different substances and it is this property which is used to separate them. The liquid that has the lower boiling temperature will boil first and enter the gas phase. The gas is condensed when it hits the cooler temperature of the condenser and is collected separately from the remaining liquid in the original flask.

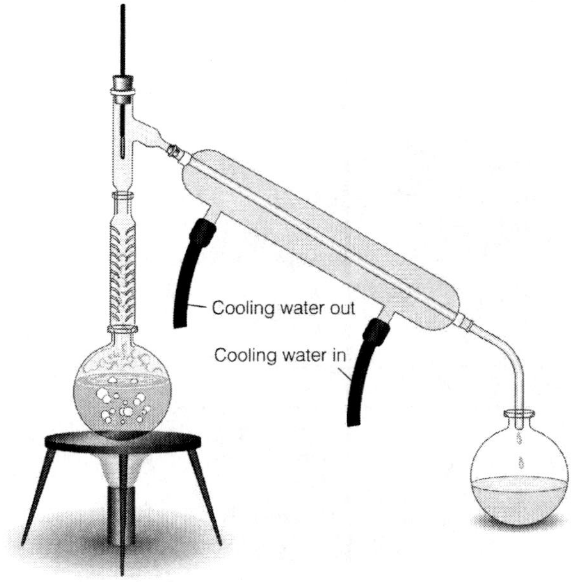

e) Gravity Separation

This method is used to separate solids in a liquid, a mechanical mixture, using the solid's different densities. A common example of this is the centrifuge which spins at extremely high speeds causing solids in the liquid to collect on the bottom of a tube with the most dense solids being on the bottom and the less dense solids on top.

f) Chromatography

This method is used to separate coloured solids which are in solution with a liquid. Absorbent material, such as paper or talc – a silica based product, is placed in the solvent and the solvent with the dissolved solids is absorbed by the material. The solids are separated by their differing abilities to dissolve in the solvent versus the absorbent material. Those that dissolve better in the absorbent material than the solvent do not travel as far up the material as those that dissolve better in the solvent than the absorbent material.

When dried, the separated solids can be separated from the absorbent material and retained as a pure substance.

2.1.4 Relate the observable properties and characteristics of elements, compounds, and mixtures to the concept of atoms and molecules

2.1.5 Define atom, molecule and ion

Atom – This is the smallest amount or quantity of an element you can have that will still retain the properties of the element.

Molecule – This is two or more atoms chemically bonded together.

Ion – This is an atom or a molecule that has an electrical charge due to the gaining or losing of an electron(s).

Related Question: 1

NOMENCLATURE

2.2.1 Write chemical symbols for elements and formulae for ions from appropriate charts

2.2.2 Name the ionic compound from a formula and write the formula given a name

2.2.3 Name the covalent compound from a formula using the prefix naming system, and write the formula given a name

2.2.4 Predict the formulae of covalent compounds given the formula of another compound containing elements in the same family (families)

2.2.5 Write the names and formulae for some common acids

Nomenclature is the terminology of chemical compounds. It is necessary to understand the language of chemistry in order to work with it.

Ionic Compound basically for naming purposes a metal ion and a non-metal ion. First is writing the formula from the name:

a) Write the symbol for the metal ion (or ammonium ion).

b) Write the symbol or formula for the non-metal or polyatomic ion.

c) Check the charge, oxidation number, of each of the ions.

d) If the charges, oxidation numbers, add up to zero then that is the formula as written.

e) If they do not add up to zero then use subscripts after the symbols so that when you multiply them by the charges the sum is zero.

Example 1

Sodium Chloride
↓ ↓
Na^{+} Cl^{-}

Sodium is +1 and Chlorine is –1 which has a sum of zero so the formula is written as **NaCl**.

Example 2

Copper I Sulphate (note Roman numeral indicates the charge on the copper)
↓ ↓
Cu^{+} SO_4^{2-}

Copper is +1 and Sulphate is – 2 so a subscript of 2 after copper would give us + 2 and then the sum would be zero. The formula is written Cu_2SO_4.

$$2Cu^{+} + SO_4^{2-} \longrightarrow Cu_2SO_4$$

Example 3

Iron III	Carbonate	(note Roman numeral indicates charge on the Iron)
↓	↓	
Fe^{3+}	CO_3^{2-}	

$$2Fe^{3+} + 3CO_3^{2-} \longrightarrow Fe_2(CO_3)_3$$

Iron is + 3 and Carbonate is – 2 so a subscript of 2 after Iron and a subscript of 3 after Carbonate would give a + 6 and a –6 with a sum of zero. The formula is written $Fe_2(CO_3)_3$.

Secondly is writing the name from the formula for Ionic Compounds:

a) Write the name of the positive ion (metal or ammonium).

b) Write the name of the negative ion.

c) If the positive is **not** in group 1 or 2, is not silver, zinc or aluminum and is not ammonium then write a Roman numeral after the name of the metal to indicate its charge (oxidation number).

Example 4

KI: K is Potassium and I is Iodide and given Potassium is in group one no Roman numeral is necessary so the name is written **Potassium Iodide**.

Example 5

YF_2 : Y is Yttrium and F is Fluoride. The fluoride has a charge of –1 and a subscript of 2 therefore a total charge of –2. We know the sum of the charges is zero which means the charge of the Yttrium must be + 2. Yttrium requires a Roman numeral to indicate charge so the formula is written Yttrium II Fluoride.

Covalent compound – for the purposes of naming, covalent compounds are composed of two non-metals chemically bonded together. The first step is to write the name from the formula:

a) Write the name of the first element.

b) If there is more than one atom of the first element present then use a prefix to indicate the number present.

c) Write the name of the second element changing its ending to "ide".

d) Use a prefix to indicate the number of atoms of the second element present.

Example 6

NO_2 : N is Nitrogen and O is Oxygen. There is one nitrogen present so we do not use a prefix with its name. There are two oxygens present so the prefix di is used to indicate the number and we change oxygen's ending to "ide". Therefore the compound is written **nitrogen dioxide**.

Example 7

P_2Cl_5 : P is Phosphorus and Cl is Chlorine. There are two phosphorus atoms present so the prefix di is used before the name. There are five chlorine atoms present so the prefix penta is used to denote this and the ending of chlorine is changed to "ide". Therefore the compound is written diphosphorus pentachloride.

Now writing the formula from the name:

a) Write the symbol of the first element named. If there is a prefix used with the name use a subscript behind the elements name to indicate the number of atoms present of the element.

b) Write the symbol for the second element named and use a subscript to indicate the number of atoms present if there are more than one.

Example 8

Sulphur dioxide: Sulphur's symbol is S. There is no prefix meaning there is one sulphur atom in the compound. Oxide means oxygen and the prefix di indicates there are two atoms of oxygen present in the compound. Therefore the compound sulphur dioxide is written SO_2.

Acids

These are the substances that have following properties

- sour taste
- corrosive in nature
- turns blue litmus to red
- the pH value is less than 7

The acids containing hydrogen and non-metallic element are written with a prefix "hydro" and suffix "ic". So, HI is called **hydro**iod**ic** acid.

If the acid contains oxygen, then the prefix comes from the anion. So, H_2CO_3 is named as carbonic acid where carbonic comes from carbonate.

ACID	NAME
HCl	Hydrochloric Acid
H_3PO_4	Phosphoric Acid
HNO_3	Nitric Acid
H_2SO_4	Sulfuric Acid

Related Questions: 3-12, WR 1

1. A molecule can be defined as

   A. two or more atoms chemically bonded together
   B. two or more elements chemically bonded together
   C. one atom capable of forming a chemical bond
   D. the smallest possible portion of a mole

2. A reasonable method of separating a suspended solid from a liquid is

   A. chromatography
   B. distillation
   C. filtration
   D. hand separation

3. Which of the following symbols represents an ion?

   A. +2
   B. Na
   C. e^-
   D. F^-

4. What is the chemical formula for Calcium Fluoride?

   A. CaF
   B. Ca_2F
   C. CaF_2
   D. Ca_2F_2

5. The chemical formula for Yttrium II Permanganate is

   A. $Y_4(MnO)_2$
   B. $Y_2(MnO_4)$
   C. $Yt(MnO_4)_2$
   D. $Y(MnO_4)_2$

6. The chemical formula for Nitrogen Dioxide is

   A. NO
   B. N_2O
   C. NO_2
   D. N_2O_2

7. What is the chemical formula for Manganese VI Phosphate?

   A. $Mn(PO)_2$
   B. $Mn(PO_4)_2$
   C. $Mn_3(PO_4)_6$
   D. $Mn(PO_4)_6$

8. What is the correct chemical name for P_2O_5?

   A. pentaPhosphorus dioxide
   B. diPhosphorus pentaoxide
   C. Phosphorus II oxide
   D. Phosphorus V oxide

CHALLENGER QUESTION

9. The correct chemical name for $Na_2SO_4 \cdot 10H_2O$ is

   A. Sodium Sulphate aqueous
   B. Sodium Sulphate hydrate
   C. Sodium Sulphate decahydrate
   D. Sodium decahydrate Sulphate

10. The proper name for CaF_2 is

A. Calcium II fluoride
B. Calcium fluoride
C. Calcium fluorine
D. Cobalt fluoride

CHALLENGER QUESTION

11. The proper name for V_2O_3 is

A. Vanadium II oxide
B. Vanadium III oxide
C. di Vanadium trioxide
D. Vanadium II oxygen

12. The chemical formula for Phosphorus trichloride is

A. PCl_3
B. P_3Cl
C. P_3Cl_3
D. Cl_3P

CHALLENGER QUESTION

13. What is the charge on the metal in the compound $Pb(CO_3)_2$?

A. – 4
B. + 2
C. + 4
D. 2

14. What is the correct chemical name for HBr?

A. Hydrochloric Acid
B. Hydrobromic Acid
C. Carbonic Acid
D. Acetic Acid

Written Response

1. **a)** Classify each of the following compounds as ionic or covalent.

i) CaF_2
ii) CO
iii) CuCl
iv) $MO_3(PO_4)_2$
v) SiF_4
vi) P_2O_5

b) Write the name of each of the above compounds.

NOTES

Mole Concept

1 Mole = 6.02×10^{23} = Number of atoms
Or
Number of molecules

↑

(Avogadro's Number)

MOLE CONCEPT

Table of Correlations			
Outcomes			**Questions**
Students are expected to:			
Introduction	3.1.1	explain the relative nature of atomic mass	
	3.1.2	identify the unit for counting atoms, molecules, or ions as the mole	
	3.1.3	define the mole	1
	3.1.4	determine the molar mass of an element or compound	2, 7
	3.1.5	perform calculations relating the number of particles, moles, and mass	3, 4, 5, 6, 8, 9
Molar Volume of Gases	3.2.1	state Avogadro's hypothesis	10, 13
	3.2.2	determine experimentally the molar volume of a gas at room temperature and pressure	
	3.2.3	state the molar volume of a gas at STP	11
	3.2.4	calculate the moles or mass of a gas from a given volume at STP or vice versa	12, WR1
Percent Composition	3.3.1	compare and contrast molecular and empirical formulae	
	3.3.2	determine the percent composition by mass from the formula of a compound	14, 15, 21
	3.3.3	determine the empirical formula for the compound from the percent composition by mass	16, 17, 22, 23, WR2
	3.3.4	determine the molecular formula from the molecular mass and empirical formula	18, 19, 20, WR3, WR4
Molarity	3.4.1	describe molarity (mol/L or M) as a measure of molar concentration	28, 24
	3.4.2	prepare a standard solution	29
	3.4.3	perform calculations relating mass (or moles) of solute, volume of solution, and molarity	25, 26, WR5, WR6
	3.4.4	calculate the resulting concentration when a given volume of a standard solution is diluted with water to a given volume	27, WR7

MOLE CONCEPT

INTRODUCTION

3.1.1 Explain the relative nature of atomic mass

3.1.2 Identify the unit for counting atoms, molecules or ions as the mole

3.1.3 Define the mole

3.1.4 Determine the molar mass of an element or compound

3.1.5 Perform calculations relating the number of particles, moles and mass

The mole is the standard unit in chemistry for communication of how much of a substance is present. Basically, a mole is the number of particles in 12 grams of carbon-12. The atomic masses of all the elements on the periodic table are relative to the mass of carbon-12. One mole of any element will contain the same number of particles as one mole of carbon-12. Atomic masses are measured in Atomic Mass Units. An atomic mass unit (amu) is defined as having 1/12 the mass of a carbon-12 atom.

The number of particles, atoms, in 12 grams of carbon-12 and thus in one mole of any element is 6.02×10^{23}. In fact, the number of particles in one mole of any substance is 6.02×10^{23}. The substance does not need to be an element and the particles do not need to be atoms. One mole of sodium chloride contains 6.02×10^{23} molecules of NaCl. One mole of anything contains 6.02×10^{23} units of the substance in question.

This is a very important concept in chemistry as it is used to relate relative quantities of any substance to any other substance. The value 6.02×10^{23} is given a name – Avogadro's number in honour of Amedeo Avogadro. Given that the atomic masses of the elements are relative to one another and one mole of carbon-12 is equal to 12 grams we can say that one mole of any element is equal to its atomic mass in grams. Then we could also say that the molar mass of any substance is equal to its molecular weight in grams.

Example 1

Determine the molar mass of Zr.

The atomic mass of Zr, Zirconium, is 91.2 amu therefore the molar mass of Zr is 91.2 g/mol.

Example 2

Calculate the molar mass of $Zn(NO_3)_2$.

This compound has

- one atom of Zinc which has a mass of 65.4 amu
- two atoms of Nitrogen each having a mass of 14.0 amu
- six atoms of Oxygen each having a mass of 16.0 amu

Recall that a mole of each element has a mass equal to its atomic mass in grams. To find the molar mass determine the total mass of all the atoms of each element in the compound:

$$(1\,\text{Zn} \times 65.4\text{ g}) + (2\,\text{N} \times 14.0\text{ g}) + (6\,\text{O} \times 16.0\text{ g}) = 189.4\text{ g/mol}$$

Example 3

Calculate the molar mass of $Pt_2O_3 \bullet 3H_2O$

$$(2\,\text{Pt} \times 195.1\text{ g}) + (3\,\text{O} \times 16.0\text{ g}) + (6\,\text{H} \times 1.0\text{ g}) + (3\,\text{O} \times 16.0g)$$

$$= 492.2\text{ g/mol}$$

Calculations involving particles, mole and mass

a) Moles to grams

Multiply moles by number of grams in a mole of the substance.

Example

Calculate the mass of 0.550 moles of NaOH.

$$0.550\text{ mol} \times \frac{40\text{ g}}{1\text{ mol}} = 22.0\text{ g NaOH}$$

b) Grams to moles

Divide mass by number of grams in a mole.

Example

Calculate the number of moles in 34.5g HCl.

$$34.5 \text{ g HCl} \times \frac{1 \text{ mol}}{36.5 \text{ g}} = 0.945 \text{ mol HCl}$$

c) Moles to particles

Multiply moles by the number of particles in a mole.

Example

Calculate the number of molecules in 1.3×10^{12} moles of H_2O.

$$1.3 \times 10^{12} \text{mol } H_2O \times \frac{(6.02 \times 10^{23} \text{ molecules})}{1 \text{ mol}}$$

$$= 7.8 \times 10^{35} \text{molecules } H_2O$$

d) Particles to moles

Divide particles by the number of particles in a mole.

Example

Calculate the number of moles in 3.550×10^{19} molecules of $CaCl_2$.

$$3.550 \times 10^{19} \text{molecules} \times \frac{1 \text{ mol}}{6.02 \times 10^{23} \text{ molecules}}$$

$$= 5.897 \times 10^{-5} \text{mol } CaCl_2$$

e) Mass to particles: these sort of calculations require a conversion first to moles and then to the second unit.

Divide mass by molar mass then multiply be number of particles in a mole.

Example

Calculate the number of atoms in 23.5 g Ag.

$$23.5 \text{ g Ag} \times \frac{1 \text{ mol}}{107.9 \text{ g}} \times \frac{6.02 \times 10^{23} \text{ atoms}}{1 \text{ mol}}$$

$$= 1.31 \times 10^{23} \text{ atoms Ag}$$

f) Particles to mass:

Divide molecules present by number of molecules in a mole then multiply by molar mass of $AgNO_3$.

Example

Calculate the mass of 2.54×10^{15} molecules of $AgNO_3$.

$$2.54 \times 10^{15} \text{ molecules} \times \frac{1 \text{ mol}}{6.02 \times 10^{23} \text{ molecules}} \times \frac{169.9 \text{ g}}{1 \text{ mol}}$$

$$= 7.17 \times 10^{-7} \text{ g } AgNO_3$$

Related Questions: 1-9

MOLAR VOLUME OF GASES

3.2.1 State Avogadro's hypothesis

3.2.2 Determine experimentally the molar volume of a gas at room temperature and pressure

3.2.3 State the molar volume of a gas at STP

3.2.4 Calculate moles or mass of a gas from a given volume at STP or visa versa

Avogadro's hypothesis states that:

Equal volumes of different gases, at the same temperature and pressure, contain the same number of particles.

Now we can state that one mole of any gas at STP occupies 22.4 L. STP is standard temperature and pressure which is equal to 0°C and 101.3 kPa.

Example

The molar volume of $H_{2(g)}$ = 22.4 L at STP.

The molar volume of $CO_{2(g)}$ = 22.4 L at STP

Thus the molar volume of $H_{2(g)}$ = the molar volume of $CO_{2(g)}$ = 22.4 L at STP

Calculations

i) Moles to volume: Multiply moles present by the number of litres in a mole at STP.

Example

Calculate the volume of 3.00 mol $O_{2(g)}$.

$$3.00\,\text{mol}\ O_{2(g)} \times \frac{22.4\,\text{L}}{1\,\text{mol}} = 67.2\,\text{L}\ O_{2(g)}$$

ii) Volume to moles: Divide the volume by the number of litres in a mole.

Example

Calculate the number of moles in 9.75 L $F_{2(g)}$.

$$9.75\,\text{L}\ F_{2(g)} \times \frac{1\,\text{mol}}{22.4\,\text{L}} = 0.435\,\text{mol}$$

iii) Volume to mass: In this conversion it is necessary to first determine number of moles and then the mass. We cannot convert directly from volume to mass but can convert any measurable unit to moles and moles to any measurable unit.

Example

Calculate the mass of 15.9 L $Cl_{2(g)}$.

$$15.9\,\text{L}\ Cl_{2(g)} \times \frac{1\,\text{mol}}{22.4\,\text{L}} \times \frac{71.0\,\text{g}}{1\,\text{mol}}$$

$$= 50.4\,\text{g}\ Cl_{2(g)}$$

iv) Mass to volume: As with the last example we cannot convert directly to volume from mass but first must determine moles.

Example

Determine the volume occupied by 100.0g $NO_{(g)}$.

$$100.0\,\text{g}\ NO_{(g)} \times \frac{1\,\text{mol}}{30.0\,\text{g}} \times \frac{22.4\,\text{L}}{1\,\text{mol}}$$

$$= 74.67\,\text{L}\ NO_{(g)}$$

Related Questions: 10-13, WR1

PERCENT COMPOSITION

3.3.1 Compare and contrast molecular and empirical formulae

3.3.2 Determine the percent composition by mass from the formula of a compound

3.3.3 Determine the empirical formula for the compound from the percent composition by mass

3.3.4 Determine the molecular formula from the molecular mass and the empirical formula

Molecular formula

The molecular formula is the true chemical formula of any given substance. The subscripts in the formula tell the actual number of atoms of each element in the compound.

Empirical formula

This is the chemical formula of a substance expressed in the lowest possible whole number ratio. The subscripts do not necessarily indicate the actual number of atoms of each element in the compound. It is possible that the empirical formula and the molecular formula of a substance are the same. For example the compound $C_3H_6O_3$ would be expressed as CH_2O.

Percent composition

This is the percent by mass of each element in the compound.

Determining percent composition

Steps

1 Determine the molar mass of the compound from its formula.

2 Determine the sum of the masses of each element by multiplying the molar mass of the element by the subscript.

3 Divide the mass attributed to each element by the molar mass of the compound and then multiply this value by 100 to get the percent.

Example

The example will be HNO_3, Nitric acid.

The molar mass of HNO_3 = 63.0g/mol. There is one Hydrogen atom in the compound with a molar mass of H = 1.0g/mol.
There is one atom of Nitrogen in the compound with a molar mass of N = 14.0g/mol. Finally, there are three atoms of Oxygen in the compound having a combined molar mass of $3 \times 16.0\text{g/mol} = 48.0$ g.

To find the percent composition by mass you divide the molar mass total of each element by the molar mass of the entire compound and multiply by 100.

% composition by mass of H –	1.0 g/63.0g $\times 100 = 1.59\%$
% composition by mass of N –	14.0 g/63.0g $\times 100 = 22.2\%$
% composition by mass of O –	48.0 g/63.0g $\times 100 = 76.2\%$

Determination of the empirical formula (from percent composition)

Steps

1 Change the percent composition by mass into a mass for each element.

2 Determine the moles of each element from the mass.

3 Determine the ratio of the elements to one another by dividing the number of moles of each by the one with the smallest value.

4 Ensure that the ratio numbers are whole – these represent the subscripts for each element in the empirical formula.

Example

A compound is known to be composed of carbon and hydrogen. The percent composition by mass of the compound is C 80.0% and H 20.0%. Calculate its empirical formula.

Step 1

Assume there is 100g of the substance so then there would be 80.0 g C and 20.0 g H.

Step 2

$$80.0\text{g C} \times \frac{1\text{mol}}{12.0\text{g}} = 6.67\text{ mol C}$$

$$20.0\text{g H} \times \frac{1\text{mol}}{1.0\text{g}} = 20.0\text{ mol H}$$

Step 3

$$\frac{6.67}{6.67} = 1\text{ C}$$

$$\frac{20}{6.67} = 3\text{ H}$$

Step 4

So there is **1C:3 H** ratio therefore the Empirical Formula is CH_3.

Example

A compound is known to be 73.72% C, 5.12% H, 4.78% N and 16.38% O. Determine the empirical formula for the compound.

Step 1

Assume there is 100g of the substance so then there would be 73.72g C, 5.12g H, 4.78g N and 16.38g O.

Step 2

$$73.12\,\text{g C} \times \frac{1\,\text{mol}}{12.01\,\text{g}} = 6.14\,\text{mol C}$$

$$5.12\,\text{g H} \times \frac{1\,\text{mol}}{1.01\,\text{g}} = 5.11\,\text{mol H}$$

$$4.78\,\text{g N} \times \frac{1\,\text{mol}}{14.01\,\text{g}} = 0.341\,\text{mol N}$$

$$16.38\,\text{g O} \times \frac{1\,\text{mol}}{16.00\,\text{g}} = 1.02\,\text{mol O}$$

Step 3

6.14/0.341 = 18 C

5.11/0.341 = 15 H

0.341/0.341 = 1 N

1.02/0.341 = 3

Step 4

So there is a 18 C:15 H: 1 N:3 O ratio therefore the Empirical formula is $C_{18}H_{15}NO_3$.

Example

A substance is known to be composed of 69.9% Fe and 30.1% O. Calculate the empirical formula of the compound.

Step 1

Assume there is 100g of the compound so there would be 69.9g Fe and 30.1g O.

Step 2

$$69.9\,\text{g Fe} \times \frac{1\,\text{mol}}{55.8\,\text{g}} = 1.25\,\text{mol Fe}$$

$$30.1\,\text{g O} \times \frac{1\,\text{mol}}{16.0\,\text{g}} = 1.88\,\text{mol O}$$

Step 3

1.25/1.25 = 1 Fe

1.88/1.25 = 1.5 O

This is not a whole number and so multiply both ratio values by a number that will make this value whole = 2.

So $1\,\text{Fe} \times 2 = 2$ and $1.5\,\text{O} \times 2 = 3$

This gives us 2 Fe: 3 O and the empirical formula will be Fe_2O_3.

Expansion: Combustion Analysis

Combustion analysis is predominantly for hydrocarbons (organic compounds). The procedure requires you to burn the hydrocarbon and trap the gases produced by the burning. The information this yields will allow you to calculate the empirical formula of the substance.

Example

A 0.500 g sample of a hydrocarbon undergoes combustion in excess pure oxygen to produce 1.69 g of CO_2 and 0.346 g of H_2O.

Step 1

Determine the mass of C you have in the CO_2 and the mass of H you have in the H_2O.

$$C \rightarrow 1.69\,\text{g} \times \frac{12.011\,\text{g C}}{44.0098\,\text{g CO}_2} = 0.4612\,\text{g C}$$

$$H \rightarrow 0.346\,\text{g} \times \frac{2.0158\,\text{g H}}{18.0152\,\text{g H}_2\text{O}} = 0.03872\,\text{g H}$$

Step 2-4

Step 2-4 is the same as the standard empirical formula procedure.

$$0.4612\,\text{g C} \times \frac{1\,\text{mol}}{12.011\,\text{g C}} = 0.03840\,\text{mol}$$

$$C/0.03840 = 1$$

$$0.03872\,\text{g H} \times \frac{1\,\text{mol}}{1.0079\,\text{g H}} = 0.03842\,\text{mol}$$

$$H/0.03840 = 1$$

1C:1H therefore empirical formula is CH.

Determination of molecular formula (from empirical formula and molar mass)

Now recall that the molecular formula is the true chemical formula of the compound and not the lowest ratio like the empirical formula. In order to determine the molecular formula you require two pieces of information, the empirical formula and the molar mass of the compound.

To determine the molecular formula use the following procedure:

$(\text{mass of empirical formula})_n = \text{molar mass of compound}$

solve for n by $n = \dfrac{\text{molar mass of compound}}{\text{mass of empirical formula}}$

Then multiply n in against the subscripts in the empirical formula to get the molecular formula.

$(\text{empirical formula})_n = \text{molecular formula}$

Example

The empirical formula of a substance is CH and its molar mass is 78.0g. Determine the molecular formula of the compound.

$(13.0\text{ g})_n = 78.0\text{g}$ therefore $n = 78.0\text{ g}/13.0\text{ g} = 6$

$(CH)_6 = C_6H_6$

Example

The empirical formula of a compound (glucose) is CH_2O and its molar mass is 180.0g. Determine the molecular formula of the compound glucose.

$(30.0\text{ g})_n = 180.0\text{ g}$ therefore n = 180.0 g/30.0 g = 6

$(CH_2O)_6 = C_6H_{12}O_6$

Related Questions: 14-23, WR2, WR3, WR4

MOLARITY

3.4.1 Describe molarity as (mol/L or M) as a measure of molar concentration

3.4.2 Prepare a standard solution

3.4.3 Perform calculations relating mass (or moles) of solute, volume of solution and molarity

3.4.4 Calculate the resulting concentration when a given volume of a standard solution is diluted with water to a given volume

Molarity is describing the concentration of a solute in solution. It is a measure of the amount of moles of solute in solution per litre of solvent. It is applied primarily with liquid solutions and with gases. The units of molarity are mol/L or simply M. Square brackets can also be used to indicate concentration, [ ].

$$\text{Molarity (M)}\,\frac{\text{Moles of solute}}{\text{Litres of solvent}}$$

Sample molarity calculations

Example

Determine the molarity of a solution produced by dissolving 1.55×10^{-3} mol KCl in 2.00L water.

$$M = \frac{\text{mol}}{\text{L}} = \frac{1.55\times10^{-3}\text{ mol}}{2.00\text{ L}} = 7.75\times10^{-4}\text{ M KCl}$$

Example

13.5g of NaCl is put into solution with 2.50L of water. Determine the [NaCl] or concentration NaCl or molarity NaCl.

First the mass NaCl must be converted into moles of NaCl. Secondly the moles of NaCl will be divided by the volume of water to determine the molarity of the NaCl.

$$13.5\text{g NaCl}\times\frac{1\text{ mol}}{58.5\text{ g}} = 0.230\text{ mol NaCl then}$$

$$M = \frac{\text{mol}}{\text{L}} = \frac{0.230\text{ mol}}{2.50\text{ L}} = 0.092\text{M NaCl}$$

This procedure can be integrated into one formula

$MV = \dfrac{\text{grams}}{\text{molar mass}}$ where M is molarity and V is Volume.

So to do the example: $M(2.50\,L)=\dfrac{13.5\,g}{58.5\,g}$

To solve for molarity: M = (13.5 g/58.5 g)/2.50 L
= 0.092 M NaCl

Example

How many grams of $KMnO_4$ would be required to produce 0.400 L of a 0.200M $KMnO_4$ solution?

Use the formula $MV=\dfrac{\text{grams}}{\text{molar mass}}$

$$(0.200\,M)(0.400\,L)=\frac{\text{grams } KMnO_4}{158.0\,g}\rightarrow$$

$$\text{grams } KMnO_4=(0.200\,M)(0.400\,L)(158.0\,g)$$

$$\text{grams } KMnO_4=12.6\,g\ KMnO_4$$

Dilution calculations with molarity

The dilution formula is $M_iV_i=M_fV_f$ where M is molarity, V is volume, *i* is initial and *f* is final.

Example

Determine the new concentration of KI if 15.0mL of water is added to 50.0mL of a 0.250M KI solution.

$M_i=0.250\,M$

$V_i=0.0500\,L$

$M_f=?$

$V_f=0.0500\,L+0.0150\,L$

$=0.0650\,L$

$(0.250\,M)(0.0500\,L)$

$=M_f(0.0650\,L)$

$$M_f=\frac{(0.250\,M)(0.0500\,L)}{(0.0650\,L)}$$

$=0.192$ M KI

V_f – the final volume was determined by combining the initial volume of the solution with the water added.

Example

Determine the volume of water that is required to dilute 1.250 L of 0.0100 M HCl to 0.00340 M HCl.

$M_i=0.0100\,M$

$V_i=1.250\,L$

$M_f=0.00340\,M$

$V_f=?$

In this problem we must first determine the final volume of the solution after is has been diluted. To then determine the volume of water added we would subtract the initial volume from the final volume.

$$(0.0100\,M)(1.25\,L)=(0.00340M)V_f$$

$$V_f=(0.0100m)(1.25L)/0.00340=3.67$$

Volume added

$=V_f-V_i=3.67\,L-1.250\,L=2.42\,L$

Steps for preparing and diluting solutions

Since all of the solution concentration units are based on volume of solution, as opposed to volume of solvent, it is necessary to use special volumetric glassware and proper technique to prepare a solution of precise concentration. This also applies to diluting solutions.

What are the correct steps for preparing 100.0 mL of a 0.100 mol/L solution of NH_4Cl?

a) Calculate the mass of NH_4Cl required: (this will be shown using unit analysis and formula methods):

Unit Analysis

$0.100\,\text{mol/L}\times0.1000\,L\times53.50\,\text{g/mol}$
$=0.535$ g

Formula

$n=c\times v$

$=0.100\,\text{mol/L}\times0.1000\,L$
$=0.535$ g

$m=n\times M$

$=0.0100\,\text{mol}\times53.50$ g/mol
$=0.535$ g

b) Using a balance, measure 0.535 g of NH_4Cl into a 100 mL beaker.

c) Add approximately 40 mL of water to the NH_4Cl in the beaker and stir to dissolve. If the solute will not completely dissolve, you may go as high as 60 mL of water, but try not to exceed this limit. Do not remove your stirring rod from the beaker.

d) Pour the NH_4Cl solution through a funnel into a 100.0 mL volumetric flask. Wash the beaker, stirring rod, and funnel into the volumetric flask using a distilled water rinse bottle.

e) Add additional distilled water to make the water's meniscus sit on the 100.0 mL mark on the volumetric flask.

f) Put a stop in the flask and invert to mix.

Sometimes it is necessary to prepare solutions by dilution. This will be necessary when the required mass of solute is too small to measure to the correct degree of precision on your balance. It is also necessary when you have a solution of precise concentration which is too high and must be diluted.

What are the correct steps for diluting a commercially available 0.500 mol/L $Fe(NO_3)_{3(aq)}$ solution to prepare 100 mL of 0.150 mol/L necessary for an experiment?

a) Calculate the volume of concentrated solution necessary for the dilution. Students generally prefer to use the formula $c_i \times v_i = c_f \times v_f$ for this calculation, where c_i and v_i are the initial concentration and volume and c_f and v_f are the final concentration and volume.

$$c_i \times v_i = c_f \times v_f$$

$$0.500\,\text{mol/L} \times v_i = 0.150\,\text{mol/L} \times 100\,\text{mL}$$

$$v_i = \frac{0.150\,\text{mol/L} \times 100\,\text{mL}}{0.500\,\text{mol/L}} = 30.0\,\text{mL}$$

b) Use a graduated pipette to obtain the 30.0 mL of concentrated solution by pouring approximately 50 mL into a 100 mL beaker. Rinse the pipette with a small volume of solution and discard this solution. Fill the pipet using a rubber bulb to beyond the 30 mL mark and dispense 30 mL of this solution into a clean 100.0 mL volumetric flask.

c) Add distilled water to the line on the volumetric flask.

d) Put a stop in the flask and invert to mix.

Note: When diluting a concentrated acid you need to put slightly less than the required volume of water into the flask before adding the concentrated acid. Once the acid is partially diluted, the remaining water can be added. Also, it is a good idea, particularly with sulfuric acid, not to invert and mix until the solution is cooled down. (You will also notice that the solution volume will decrease as the temperature drops. Volumetric flasks are calibrated at 20°C.)

Related Questions: 24-27, WR5, WR6, WR7

1. A mole can be defined as

A. the number of carbon atoms in 12g of carbon-12
B. the number of carbon atoms in 12g of carbon-13
C. the number of carbon atoms in 12g of carbon
D. the number of atoms in 12g of the average mass of carbon

2. What is the mass of 2.00 moles of Sodium?

A. 11.5 g
B. 23.0 g
C. 46.0 g
D. 46 g

3. How many moles are in 32.0g of CO_2?

A. 1400 mol
B. 1.38 mol
C. 0.73 mol
D. 0.727 mol

4. How many molecules are present in 1.50 moles of NaCl?

A. 2.49×10^{-24}
B. 9×10^{23}
C. 9.03×10^{23}
D. 9.30×10^{23}

5. How many moles of Gold (Au) are in 4.55×10^{30} atoms of Gold?

A. 1.32×10^{-7} mol
B. 7.56×10^{6} mol
C. 7.65×10^{6} mol
D. 2.74×10^{54} mol

6. How many molecules are in 10.0g of KCl?

A. 8.07×10^{22} molecules

B. 8.07×10^{-22} molecules

C. 4.49×10^{26} molecules

D. 2.23×10^{-25} molecules

CHALLENGER QUESTION

7. What is the mass of 1.00×10^{-6} mol $CaCl_2$?

A. 9.00×10^{-9} g $CaCl_2$

B. 1.111×10^{-4} g $CaCl_2$

C. 1.11×10^{-5} g $CaCl_2$

D. 1.11×10^{-4} g $CaCl_2$

CHALLENGER QUESTION

8. How many moles of PCl_3 are present in 1.55×10^{45} molecules of PCl_3?

A. 2.57×10^{21} moles of PCl_3

B. 9.33×10^{33} moles of PCl_3

C. 2.57×10^{11} moles of PCl_3

D. 5.27×10^{21} moles of PCl_3

9. What is the mass of 584 atoms of Au?

A. 4.92×10^{-24} g Au

B. 6.93×10^{28} g Au

C. 1.91×10^{-19} g Au

D. 1.78×10^{24} g Au

10. Avogadro's hypothesis states that

A. equal volumes of different gases, at the same temperature and pressure, contain the same number of particles

B. equal volumes of different gases, at different temperature and pressure, contain the same number of particles

C. proportionate volumes of different gases, at the same temperature and pressure, contain equal numbers of particles

D. equal volumes of varying gases, at similar temperatures and pressures, contain the same number of particles

11. At STP, the molar volume of any gas is

A. 22.2 L

B. 22.4 L

C. 24.2 L

D. 24.4 L

12. What volume does 10.0 moles of $F_{2(g)}$ occupy?

A. 0.410 L

B. 0.446 L

C. 224 L

D. 244 L

13. What is the mass of 50.0L of $O_{2(g)}$?

A. 26.6 g

B. 35.7 g

C. 65.5 g

D. 71.4 g

14. What is the percent composition of chlorine in PCl_5?

A. 14%

B. 17%

C. 60%

D. 85%

CHALLENGER QUESTION

15. What is the percent composition of $KMnO_4$?

A. 34.7% K, 24.7% Mn, 40.5% O
B. 24.7% K, 34.7% Mn, 40.5% O
C. 14.7% K, 44.7% Mn, 40.5% O
D. 42.7% K, 34.7% Mn, 22.6% O

16. Jacqueline analyzed a compound and found it to be 52.7% Potassium and 47.3% Chlorine. She determined the empirical formula to be

A. KCl
B. KCl_2
C. K_2Cl
D. K_2Cl_2

17. Sonia analyzed a compound and found that it contained 53.7% iron and 46.3% sulphur. She determined the empirical formula to be

A. FeS
B. Fe_2S_3
C. FeS_2
D. Fe_3S_2

18. The empirical formula of a compound is NO_2. Given its molar mass is 92.0 g, its molecular formula would be

A. N_2O_4
B. N_4O_2
C. N_4O_6
D. NO_2

19. Given the empirical formula of a compound is CH_2 and its molar mass is 70.0 g, its molecular formula would be

A. C_3H_6
B. C_4H_8
C. C_4H_{10}
D. C_5H_{10}

20. A compound was analyzed and found to be 92.3% C and 7.7% H with a molar mass of 78.0g. Its molecular formula would be

A. C_6H_6
B. C_3H_5
C. CH_3
D. CH

21. What is the percent composition of the water in bold in $Al_2(SO_3)_3{\bullet}16H_2O$?

A. 3.09%
B. 5.83%
C. 49.5%
D. 64.5%

22. Which of the following is the empirical formula for a compound that is 13.0% Mg and 87.0% Br.

A. MgBr
B. Mg_2Br
C. $MgBr_2$
D. Mg_2Br_2

CHALLENGER QUESTION

23. Determine the empirical formula for a compound that is 25.3% Cu, 12.9% S, 25.7% O and 36.1% H_2O.

A. $Cu(SO_4)_2{\bullet}5H_2O$
B. $CuSO_4{\bullet}5H_2O$
C. $Cu(SO_4)_2{\bullet}H_2O$
D. $CuSO_4{\bullet}H_2O$

24. Molarity is a measure of

A. moles per mass
B. molar volume
C. molar concentration
D. molar activity

25. If 0.15 mol NaCl goes into solution with 2.00 L water, the molarity of NaCl is

A. 0.500M NaCl
B. 0.30M NaCl
C. 0.075M NaCl
D. 0.0050M NaCl

26. If 20.5g of NaOH is dissolved in 0.950 L water, the molarity of NaOH is

A. 0.539M NaOH
B. 0.0539M NaOH
C. 0.487M NaOH
D. 0.0487M NaOH

27. If 100.0mL water is added to 150.0 mL of a 2.00M HCl solution, the new molarity of HCl is

A. 1.20M HCl
B. 0.120M HCl
C. 3.00M HCl
D. 0.0300M HCl

28. The **best** way to prepare 100 mL of 0.0400 mol/L $HCl_{(aq)}$ from a standard 0.200 mol/L $HCl_{(aq)}$ solution is to

A. use a burette and transfer 20.0 mL of 0.200 mol/L $HCl_{(aq)}$ to a 100 mL Erlenmeyer flask and then top up the solution volume to the 100 mL line with distilled water. Finally, stopper the flask and invert it several times to mix the contents thoroughly.
B. use a volumetric pipette and transfer 20.0 mL of 0.200 mol/L $HCl_{(aq)}$ to a 100 mL volumetric flask and then top up the solution volume to the calibration mark with distilled water. Finally, put a stop in the flask and invert it several times to mix the contents thoroughly.
C. measure 20 mL of 0.200 mL/L $HCl_{(aq)}$ in a 100 mL volumetric cylinder and then top up the solution volume to 100 mL with distilled water.
D. dissolve 20 mL of 0.200 mol/L $HCl_{(aq)}$ in exactly 80 mL of distilled water in a beaker and then swirl the mixture to thoroughly mix the solution.

29. Which of the following techniques is the **best** way of preparing 100 mL of a 0.0500 mol/L sodium carbonate $Na_2CO_{3(aq)}$ standard solution?

A. Carefully pipette 10 mL of a 0.0500 mol/L sodium carbonate stock solution into a 100 mL volumetric flask and then add water to the 100 mL mark.

B. Carefully pour 0.500 mol/L sodium carbonate stock solution into a 100 mL graduated cylinder to the 10 mL mark then add water to the 100 mL mark.

C. Dissolve 0.530 g of solid sodium carbonate in a 200 mL beaker, add water to the 100 mL mark, then carefully transfer the solution to a 100 mL volumetric flask.

D. In a 50 mL beaker, dissolve 0.530 g of solid calcium carbonate in deionized water, carefully transfer the solution to a 100 mL volumetric flask, then add water to the 100 mL mark.

Written Response

1. What is the mass of $N_{2(g)}$ in a $30\,m^3$ room filled with the gas at STP?

2. Determine the percent by mass composition of all the elements in $Ag(NH_3)_2F$.

3. A compound has an empirical formula of NO_2 and a molar mass of 92.0 g. Determine its molecular formula.

4. A compound is known to be 40.0% C, 6.7% H and 53.5% O with a molar mass of 60.0 g. Determine the compound's molecular formula.

5. Calculate the molarity of a solution produced by dissolving 7.45×10^{-2} g K_2O in 340.0 mL of water.

6. What mass of NaCl is required to produce 200.0 mL of a 0.500 M NaCl solution?

7. Billal had 47.0 L of 0.250 M Na_2SO_4. He wants to dilute the solution to 0.125 M. Calculate the volume of water he must add to the solution in order to do the dilution.

Chemical Reactions

CHEMICAL REACTIONS

Table of Correlations		
Outcomes		**Questions**
Students are expected to:		
Introduction	4.1.1 define reactants and products	1
	4.1.2 observe and record changes that occur during a chemical reaction	
	4.1.3 describe chemical reactions in terms of the rearrangement of the atoms as bonds are broken and new bonds are formed	
	4.1.4 gather experimental data that lead to the Law of Conservation of Mass	2
	4.1.5 apply the Law of Conservation of Mass to a formula equation of a reaction to demonstrate that atoms are conserved in the reaction	
	4.1.6 balance formula equations of several chemical reactions	
	4.1.7 use subscripts to represent solids, liquids, gases, and aqueous solutions	8, 9, 14, 16, 19, 20
	4.1.8 classify, predict products, and write balanced equations for the following types of chemical reactions: • synthesis • decomposition • single replacement • double replacement • combustion • acid-base neutralization	3, 4, 5, 10, 11, 13, 15, 17, 18, NR1
	4.1.9 define exothermic and endothermic reactions	
	4.1.10 classify reactions as exothermic or endothermic based on experimental observations	6,7
	4.1.11 relate energy changes to bond breaking and formation	
	4.1.12 write equations for chemical reactions including the energy term	
Stoichiometry	4.2.1 relate the coefficients in a balanced equation to the relative number of molecules or moles (the mole ratio) of reactants and products in the chemical reaction	
	4.2.2 perform calculations involving reactions using any of the following: • number of molecules • moles • mass • gas volume at STP • solution concentration and volume	12, 21, 22, 24, 25, 26, 27
	4.2.3 perform calculations involving limiting reagent	23, WR1

CHEMICAL REACTIONS

INTRODUCTION

4.1.1 Define reactants and products

4.1.2 Observe and record changes that occur during a chemical reaction

4.1.3 Describe chemical reactions in terms of the rearrangement of the atoms as bonds are broken and new bonds are formed

4.1.4 Gather experimental data that lead to the law of conservation of mass

4.1.5 Apply the law of conservation of mass to a formula equation of a reaction to demonstrate that atoms are conserved in the reaction

4.1.6 Balance formula equations of several chemical equations

4.1.7 Use subscripts to represent solids, liquids, gases, and aqueous solutions

4.1.8 Classify, predict products and write balanced equations for the following types of chemical equations: synthesis, decomposition, single replacement, double replacement, combustion, acid-base neutralization

4.1.9 Define exothermic and endothermic reactions

4.1.10 Classify reactions as exothermic or endothermic based on experimental observations

4.1.11 Relate energy changes to bond breaking and formation

4.1.12 Writing equations for chemical reactions including the energy term

A chemical reaction has two important elements, the **reactants** and the **products**. The reactants are the substances which are actually undergoing a chemical change while the products are the substances produced by the chemical change. The coefficients in a balanced chemical reaction tell us in what ratio the reactants are used and the products are formed. Also involved in any chemical reaction is an energy change. The reaction will either absorb energy or release energy. If the reaction absorbs energy it is termed an endothermic reaction and if the reaction releases energy it is termed an exothermic reaction.

The chemical reaction involves the chemical bonds between the reactants breaking apart, this requires energy, and then reforming new bonds, this releases energy, to form new substances with new properties. A chemical reaction is like a pile of lego pieces that are taken apart and rearranged in a new order. The products are composed of the same atoms the reactants were composed of which have been rearranged in a new order thus forming new substances with new properties.

Reactants → Products or Reactants yield Products

The **Law of Conservation of Mass** describes the above concept of the reactants forming the products. It simply states that the mass of the products will be equal to the mass of the reactants that formed them. This makes sense as the atoms of the reactants are the atoms that form the products. Now this law is not strictly true as there is a slight conversion of mass into energy so in fact a tiny amount of mass is lost in the chemical reaction. There is another law called the Law of conservation of mass-energy to account for this but it is beyond the scope of the course.

The coefficients tell us the numbers of molecules or atoms which are involved in the reaction. The coefficients also tell us the numbers of moles which are involved in the reaction. Consider the following:

$$Zn + 2HCl \rightarrow ZnCl_2 + H_2$$

The coefficients tell us that one mole of Zinc is reacting with two moles of Hydrochloric acid to produce one mole of Zinc Chloride and one mole of Hydrogen.

The mole ratios in balanced chemical reaction equations provide quantitative information about substances.

In a balanced chemical equation, the coefficients (the numbers in front of each chemical entity) give an indication of the relative amounts (numbers of moles) of each substance in the chemical reaction.

Consider the following example:

$$2C_4H_{10(g)} + 13O_{2(g)} \rightarrow 8CO_{2(g)} + 10H_2O_{(g)}$$

The coefficients are 2, 13, 8, and 10 respectively. The equation could be read 2 moles of $C_4H_{10(g)}$

+ 13 moles of $O_{2(g)}$ produces 8 moles of

$CO_{2(g)}$

10 moles of $H_2O_{(g)}$

Likewise the mole ratios will be useful in calculating numbers of moles from a starting number. The mole ratio of $C_4H_{10(g)}$ to $CO_{2(g)}$ is $\frac{2}{8}$ or $\frac{1}{4}$.

In other words there are 4 times as many moles of $CO_{2(g)}$ as there are of $C_4H_{10(g)}$.

Given that the Law of Conservation is being followed and we know the atoms of the reactants form the products it is important to be able to balance a chemical reaction. The balanced equation will have equal numbers of each atom of each element on both sides of the reaction: reactants and products. It is with coefficients that we balance the reaction. The coefficients can only be placed in front of the chemical formula representing the reactants and products.

Example

$$KClO_3 \rightarrow KCl + O_2$$

This reaction is not balanced, it is a skeleton reaction. The reactants contain one atom of potassium, one atom of chlorine and three atoms of oxygen while the products contain one atom of potassium, one atom of chlorine and two atoms of oxygen. The oxygens are not balanced. To balance the oxygens we find a common factor being six so we will use coefficients to adjust the number of oxygens on both sides of the reaction.

$$2KClO_3 \rightarrow KCl + 3O_2$$

Now the oxygens are balanced but we have unbalanced the potassiums and chlorines. The reactant side now has two of each while the product side has one of each. We can use a coefficient of two in front of the KCl on the product side to balance this inequity.

$$2KClO_3 \rightarrow 2KCl + 3O_2$$

This reaction is now balanced with equal numbers of each atom on both the reactant and product sides of the reaction.

Predicting the products of a chemical reaction, based upon the reaction type

In Science 10, you learned 6 different reaction types. These types can be used to predict the products of simple chemical reactions. Reaction types and examples are given below

Formation or Single Replacement

element + element → compound

$$4Al_{(s)} + 3O_{2(g)} \rightarrow 2Al_2O_{3(s)}$$

Simple Decomposition

compound → element + element

$$2H_2O_{(g)} \rightarrow 2H_{2(g)} + O_{2(g)}$$

Combustion

compound + $O_{2(g)}$ → most common oxides of elements of the compound

Note: most of the time your combustion reactions will be **hydrocarbon combustions** (involving compounds of the formula C_xH_y).

The format now becomes hydrocarbon + oxygen → carbon dioxide + water vapour

$$C_3H_{8(g)} + 5O_{2(g)} \rightarrow 3CO_{2(g)} + 4H_2O_{(g)}$$

Single Replacement

element + compound → element + compound

$$Cu_{(s)} + 2AgNO_{3(aq)} \rightarrow 2Ag_{(s)} + Cu(NO_3)_{2(aq)}$$

The above example illustrates 2 points:

a) Copper can form two possible ions, Cu^{2+} or Cu^{+}. How do you know which one to use for your product? Use the more common one as indicated on your periodic table. This is Cu^{2+}. Therefore the product is $Cu(NO_3)_{2(aq)}$ as opposed to $CuNO_{3(aq)}$.

b) You will have to use your solubility chart to determine the state of your products in solution reactions. In some questions it will be necessary to know which product is the precipitate for your calculations.

Double Replacement

compound + compound → compound + compound

$$2\,NaI_{(aq)} + Pb(NO_3)_{2(aq)} \rightarrow PbI_{2(s)} + 2\,NaNO_{3(aq)}$$

Both points mentioned for single replacement reactions are likewise important here.

Other

These are reactions which do not fit the above 5 classes. At this point you have no way of predicting what will happen.

Related Questions: 1-20, NR1

STOICHIOMETRY

4.2.1 *Relate the coefficients in a balanced equation to the relative number of molecules or moles (the mole ratio) of reactants and products in the chemical reaction*

4.2.2 *Perform calculations involving reactions using any of the following:*

- *number of molecules*
- *moles*
- *mass*
- *gas volume at STP*
- *solution concentration and volume*

4.2.3 *Perform calculations involving limiting reagent*

Stoichiometry is derived from two Greek words, stoicheion meaning element and metron meaning measure. Stoichiometry is a calculation based area of chemistry which uses balanced equations to allow you to determine relative quantities of reactants to products. You can calculate how much product could be produced given known quantities of reactants or how much reactant is required to produce given amounts of product.

A very important note for any stoichiometry question is that the chemical reaction must be described by a balanced equation. The coefficients of the balanced chemical reaction relate the numbers of moles, or molecules, of reactants to one another and to the products. Consider the following:

$$2\,KClO_3 \rightarrow 2\,KCl + 3\,O_2$$

This reaction tells us 2 moles of $KClO_3$ are decomposing to produce 2 moles of KCl and 3 moles of O_2, or that 2 molecules of $KClO_3$ are decomposing to produce 2 molecules of KCl and 3 molecules of O_2. The ratios are the same as equal numbers of moles contain equal numbers of molecules. These coefficients allow us to see the molar ratios between all reactants and products and thus allow for the stoichiometric calculations.

Consider the reaction:
$4\,NH_3 + 5\,O_2 \rightarrow 6\,H_2O + 4\,NO$ for purposes of the following examples.

Example

If we have 3.00 mol of NH_3 reacting with excess O_2 how many moles of H_2O could be produced?

In a balanced chemical equation it is possible to do calculations between different chemical species providing you have the unit mole. To do the calculation multiply the moles of NH_3 by the molar ratio between NH_3 and H_2O. The numerator of the ratio is the substance you are starting with and the denominator of the ration is the substance you are calculating for.

The molar ratio will be $\frac{6\,H_2O}{4\,NH_3}$ therefore 3.00 mol

$$NH_3 \times \frac{6\,H_2O}{4\,NH_3} = 4.50 \text{ mol } H_2O$$

Example

How many molecules of O_2 are required to produce 1.500×10^{10} molecules of NO?

In this example we have a known amount of product and are asked for the amount of a reactant required to produce it. Like with moles we can do direct calculations between reactants and products using a balanced chemical equation for molecules.

$$1.500\text{x}10^{10} \text{ molecules NO} \times \frac{5O_2}{4\text{NO}} = 1.875 \times 10^{10} \text{ molecules } O_2$$

↖molar ratio

Mass to mass stoichiometry

Utilizing mass in stoichiometric calculations involves adding one or two more steps to the process. Recall we can calculate between substances in the balanced equation using the unit mole. Subsequently when using masses we must calculate its mole equivalent before doing a calculation between different chemical species in the equation.

Example 1

Calculate the mass of oxygen required to react with 8.00 g of ammonia according to the following reaction:

$$4\,NH_3 + 5\,O_2 \rightarrow 6\,H_2O + 4\,NO$$

To do these calculations first have a plan – map out the steps you must do.

Mass NH_3 → moles NH_3 → moles O_2 → mass O_2 then calculate:

$$8.00\text{g } NH_3 \times \frac{1\text{mol } NH_3}{17\text{g } NH_3} \times \frac{5O_2}{4NH_3} \times \frac{32\text{g } O_2}{1\text{mol } O_2}$$

$$= 18.8 \text{ g } O_2 \text{ required}$$

Example 2

Calculate the mass of sodium iodide required to produce 55.0 g of iodine according to the following reaction:

$$K_2Cr_2O_7 + 6NaI + 7H_2SO_4 \rightarrow$$
$$Cr_2(SO_4)_3 + 3I_2 + 7H_2O + 3Na_2SO_4 + K_2SO_4$$

Plan: mass I_2 → moles I_2 → moles NaI → mass NaI

Solution concentration and mixed problems

These problems are similar to the mass – mass questions but they are simply using different units. The procedure is the same – convert the starting unit to moles, use molar ratio to find moles of finishing substance then convert moles of finishing substance to desired unit.

Example 1

Determine the theoretical yield of sodium sulphate in grams if 500.0 mL of a 0.200 M NaI solution reacts with excess Potassium dichromate and sulphuric acid according to the following reaction:

$$K_2Cr_2O_7 + 6NaI + 7H_2SO_4 \rightarrow$$

$$Cr_2(SO_4)_3 + 3I_2 + 7H_2O + 3Na_2SO_4 + K_2SO_4$$

Plan: molarity NaI → moles NaI → moles Na_2SO_4 → mass Na_2SO_4.

$$0.200\text{M NaI} \times 0.5000\text{L} \times \frac{3\,Na_2SO_4}{6\,\text{NaI}} \times$$

$$\frac{142.1\text{g } Na_2SO_4}{1\text{mol } Na_2SO_4} = 0.711 \text{ g } Na_2SO_4$$

Stoichiometry and limiting reagents

If one reactant is completely consumed during a chemical reaction before any of the other reactants then the reaction stops and that reactant limits the yield of the products. In these sorts of problems you first determine the limiting reagent and then calculate the theoretical yield of the product(s) in question.

$$2C_2H_6 + 7O_2 \rightarrow 4CO_2 + 6H_2O$$

Example 1

Determine the limiting reagent if 2.0 moles of ethane, C_2H_6, is burned with 9.0 moles of oxygen according to the following reaction

$$2C_2H_6 + 7O_2 \rightarrow 4CO_2 + 6H_2O$$

Plan: moles C_2H_6 $\rightarrow$ moles O_2 to determine limiting reagent.

$$2.0\,\text{mol}\ C_2H_6 \times \frac{7O_2}{2C_2H_6} = 7.0\ \text{mol}\ O_2$$

We can see that if all the ethane is consumed it will have reacted with 7.0 mol O_2. There are 9.0 moles of the oxygen present in the reaction which is more than is required to react with all the Ethane. The ethane is consumed first and is thus the limiting reagent.

Example 2

Chlorine is prepared by the following reaction:

$$2KMnO_4 + 16HCl \rightarrow 2KCl + 2MnCl_2 + 8H_2O + 5Cl_2$$

Determine the theoretical volume yield at STP of Chlorine, Cl_2, if 100.0 g of potassium permanganate, $KMnO_4$, reacts with 750.0 mL of 6.00 M hydrochloric acid, HCl.

First plan: find limiting reagent.

Mass $KMnO_4$ $\rightarrow$ moles $KMnO_4$ $\rightarrow$ moles HCl $\rightarrow$ molarity HCl

$$100.0\,\text{g}\ KMnO_4 \times \frac{1\,\text{mol}\ KMnO_4}{158.0\,\text{g}\ KMnO_4} \times \frac{16\,HCl}{2\ KMnO_4}$$

= 5.06 mol HCl/0.7500 L = 6.75 M HCl

If all the $KMnO_4$ were to react, it would require 750.0 mL of 6.75 M HCl but the HCl in question is only 6.00 M thus the HCl is the limiting reagent. We calculate the theoretical yield of product from the limiting reagent.

OR

$$\frac{100\ \text{g}\ KMnO_4}{158.0\ \text{g}\ KMnO_4} = 0.633\ \text{mol}\ KMnO_4$$

$$6.00\ \text{M HCl} \times 0.7500\text{L} = 4.50\ \text{mol HCl}$$

$$\frac{2KMnO_4}{0.633\,\text{mol}} = \frac{16\,HCl}{x}$$

x = 5.06 mol HCl required

We don't have 5.06 mol of HCl to react with all the $KMnO_4$ therefore HCl is the limiting reagent.

Second Plan: determine theoretical yield of Cl_2 from the limiting reagent HCl.

Molarity HCl $\rightarrow$ moles HCl $\rightarrow$ moles Cl_2 $\rightarrow$ volume Cl_2

$$6.00\,\text{M HCl} \times 0.7500\,\text{L} \times \frac{5Cl_2}{16\,HCl} \times \frac{22.4\,\text{L}}{1\,\text{mol HCl}}$$

$$= 31.51\ \text{L HCl}$$

Related Questions: 12, 21-27, WR1

1. In a chemical reaction, the product can best be described as

A. a starting substance of the reaction
B. a variation of the reactants
C. a new substance with new properties
D. a chemical variation of a reactant

2. Given a closed system and a reaction involving no gases, if you took the masses of the reactants and the products you would expect them to be

A. close to equal
B. different
C. identical
D. similar

3. The following reaction can be identified as
$H_2O \rightarrow H_2 + O_2$

A. acid/base neutralization
B. combustion
C. decomposition
D. synthesis

4. The following reaction can be identified as
$C_3H_8O_2 \rightarrow CO_2 + H_2O$

A. synthesis
B. combustion
C. decomposition
D. single replacement

5. The following reaction can be identified as
$Al + Fe_2O_3 \rightarrow Al_2O_3 + Fe$

A. single replacement
B. double replacement
C. acid/base neutralization
D. water producing

6. Exothermic means the reaction

A. absorbs energy
B. creates energy
C. releases energy
D. transfers energy

7. The following reaction can be described as
$Mg_{(aq)} + O_{2(aq)} \rightarrow MgO_{(s)} \quad \Delta H - 285.8\,kJ$

A. synthesis and endothermic
B. synthesis and exothermic
C. combustion and endothermic
D. decomposition and exothermic

8. The coefficients for the following balanced reaction are
$KOH + H_2SO_4 \rightarrow K_2SO_4 + H_2O$

A. 4, 1, 2, 4
B. 4, 2, 1, 4
C. 2, 1, 1, 1
D. 2, 1, 1, 2

9. The coefficients for the following balanced reaction are
C4H10 + O2 → CO2 + H2O

A. 4, 26, 16, 20
B. 3, 18, 12, 15
C. 2, 13, 8, 10
D. 1, 7, 4, 5

CHALLENGER QUESTION

10. The reaction of $Ba(OH)_{2(aq)}$ and $H_2SO_{4(aq)}$ produces a precipitate with the chemical formula

A. $Ba(OH)_{2(s)}$
B. $BaSO_{4(s)}$
C. $H_2SO_{4(s)}$
D. $H_2O_{(s)}$

Use the following information to answer the next two questions.

Hydrochloric acid, $HCl_{(aq)}$, is produced in the stomach to aid in the breakdown of food. Excess stomach acid, however, can irritate the lower esophagus causing heartburn. Milk of Magnesia, a suspension of $Mg(OH)_{2(s)}$ in water, can usually provide effective relief from heartburn pain.

11. A balanced equation for the reaction of Milk of Magnesia with excess stomach acid is

A. $HCl_{(aq)} + Mg(OH)_{2(s)} \rightarrow HOH_{(l)} + MgCl_{(aq)}$

B. $HCl_{(aq)} + Mg(OH)_{2(s)} \rightarrow H_2O_{(l)} + MgCl_{(aq)}$

C. $2HCl_{(aq)} + Mg(OH)_{2(s)} \rightarrow 2HOH_{(l)} + MgCl_{2(aq)}$

D. $2HCl_{(aq)} + 2Mg(OH)_{(s)} \rightarrow HOH_{(l)} + 2MgCl_{(aq)}$

12. How many moles of stomach acid are neutralized for every mole of magnesium hydroxide in Milk of Magnesia?

A. 3
B. 1
C. 2
D. 4

Use the following information to answer the next question.

Carbon dioxide levels on board the space shuttle must be controlled in order to prevent the buildup of exhaled $CO_{2(g)}$. Canisters of LiOH are commonly used for this purpose. The unbalanced reaction that occurs is

$$LiOH_{(s)} + CO_{2(g)} \rightarrow Li_2CO_{3(s)} + H_2O_{(l)}$$

13. The mole ratio of lithium hydroxide to carbon dioxide in the balanced chemical equation is

A. 1:1
B. 1:2
C. 1:3
D. 2:1

PARTNERS IN EDUCATION

Use the following information to answer the next question.

Marijuana is second only to alcohol as the drug most frequently found in the bodies of crash victims. The Enzyme Multiplied Immunoassay Technique (EMIT) can be used to detect the presence of a particular substance in urine, serum, or plasma. The EMIT is used in laboratories to screen for the presence of illicit drugs such as marijuana, barbiturates, amphetamines, and opiates.

14. EMIT is an example of a

A. titration analysis
B. gravimetric analysis
C. quantitative analysis
D. qualitative analysis

ICBC Road Sense

Use the following information to answer the next two questions.

Sodium hydroxide has been used to make "lye soap" for centuries. The soap forms when fatty acids are heated with $NaOH_{(s)}$. Soaps made

with $NaOH_{(s)}$ usually feel hard to the touch. NaOH is also used in the chemical and pulp and paper industries.

15. The concentration of $NaOH_{(s)}$ in a soap sample was established by titrating it with $HCl_{(aq)}$. The dissolved ions present in this titration were

A. $H^+_{(aq)}, OH^-_{(aq)}$ and $Cl^-_{(aq)}$

B. $Na^+_{(aq)}, Cl^-_{(aq)}$ and $H_2O_{(l)}$

C. $H_2O_{(l)}, H^+_{(aq)}$ and $OH^-_{(aq)}$

D. $Na^+_{(aq)}, OH^-_{(aq)}, H^+_{(aq)}$ and $Cl^-_{(aq)}$

Use the following information to answer the next question.

Alchemy is the precursor of modern chemistry and metallurgy. Many alchemists tried to change baser metals into gold. Gold was believed to be the perfect metal and a key to immortality. Several "aurifaction" recipes were created. One such process, which resulted in golden crystals of tin (IV) sulfide, is shown:

#1. $KAl(SO_4)_2 \rightarrow K_2SO_4 + Al_2O_3 + SO_3$

#2. $SO_3 + 2Sn \rightarrow SnS_2 + SnO_2$

(This reaction sequence was described by the Chinese alchemist Ko Hung.)

16. When equation #1 is balanced, the mole ratio of potassium aluminum sulfate, $KAl(SO_4)_2$, to aluminum oxide, Al_2O_3, is

A. 1:1

B. 2:3

C. 1:2

D. 2:1

CHALLENGER QUESTION

17. The visible exhaust coming from the chimneys of homes during the winter is

A. water vapor that has condensed

B. methane that is unburnt

C. pollutants of combustion known as smog

D. carbon dioxide combined with other greenhouse gases

Use the following information to answer the next question.

Many gases, including carbon dioxide, contribute to the effects of global warming. Photosynthesis is a process that removes carbon dioxide gas from the atmosphere. A balanced equation for photosynthesis is shown below.

$$6\,H_2O + 6\,CO_2 \rightarrow C_6H_{12}O_6 + 6\,O_2$$

18. The photosynthesis reaction can be described as

A. decomposition

B. formation

C. endothermic

D. exothermic

Use the following information to answer the next two questions.

Limestone buildings contain large amounts of calcium carbonate. Calcium carbonate will react readily with the hydrogen ions present in acid rain to produce water, carbon dioxide, and calcium ions. The calcium may enter the water supply and contribute to the "hard water build up" sometimes observed on kettles and pots. Below is an unbalanced chemical reaction showing this process.

$$CaCO_3 + H^+ \rightarrow H_2O + CO_2 + Ca^{2+}$$

CHALLENGER QUESTION

19. The states of matter for the reactants and products, from left to right, are

A. s, aq, l, g, and aq
B. s, s, l, g, and s
C. aq, aq, l, g, and s
D. s, aq, l, g, and s

20. When the above equation is balanced, the coefficients from left to right are

A. 1, 2, 1, 1, and 1
B. 1, 4, 2, 1, and 1
C. 2, 2, 1, 2, and 2
D. 1, 1, 1, 1, and 1

Use the following information to answer the next question.

Butane, $C_4H_{10(g)}$, is commonly used in cigarette lighters. When the lighter is ignited, the following reaction takes place.

$$2C_4H_{10(g)} + 13O_{2(g)} \rightarrow 8CO_{2(g)} + 10H_2O_{(g)}$$

Numerical Response

CHALLENGER QUESTION

1. Which of the following descriptions classifies the above reaction? ____ ____ ____

Write your answer in ascending numerical order

1. A physical change
2. A chemical change
3. An endothermic reaction
4. An exothermic reaction
5. A formation reaction
6. A decomposition reaction
7. A single replacement reaction
8. A double replacement reaction
9. A combustion reaction

Use the following reaction for questions 21 to 23.

$$Cu + 2AgNO_3 \rightarrow 2Ag + Cu(NO_3)_2$$

21. One mole of Cu reacts with:

A. 2 moles of Ag
B. 2 moles of NO_3^-
C. 2 moles of $AgNO_3$
D. 2 moles of $Cu(NO_3)_2$

22. If 1.5×10^{-2} mol $AgNO_3$ reacted it could produce

A. 7.5×10^{-3} mol $Cu(NO_3)_2$
B. 1.5×10^{-2} mol $Cu(NO_3)_2$
C. 3.0×10^{-2} mol Ag
D. 7.5×10^{-3} mol Cu

23. 1.8 mol Cu and 2.9 mol $AgNO_3$ are placed in a reaction vessel. The limiting reagent in this case is

A. $AgNO_3$

B. Ag

C. $Cu(NO_3)_2$

D. Cu

24. Consider the following reaction
$2\,KNO_3 \rightarrow 2\,KNO_2 + O_2$
If 0.500 mol KNO_3 were to react, the volume of O_2 produced would be

A. 2.24 L

B. 5.60 L

C. 0.560 L

D. 0.0446 L

25. Consider the following reaction:
$2\,HCl + Ca(OH)_2 \rightarrow 2\,H_2O + CaCl_2$
If 25.0 g of $Ca(OH)_2$ were to react, the mass of H_2O produced would be

A. 0.112 g

B. 1.01 g

C. 12.1 g

D. 40.1 g

26. Consider the following reaction:
$AgNO_{3(aq)} + NaCl_{(aq)} \rightarrow AgCl_{(s)} + NaNO_{3(aq)}$
If 10.0 mL of 0.200 M NaCl were to react, the mass of AgCl produced would be

A. 0.0287 g

B. 0.287 g

C. 2.87 g

D. 287 g

Use the following information to answer the next question.

Silverware commonly tarnishes and needs to be polished clean. The tarnish is silver sulphide, Ag_2S.

27. What mass of Ag_2S could be produced from 0.0255 g H_2S according to the following reaction?

$$4\,Ag + 2\,H_2S + O_2 \rightarrow 2\,Ag_2S + 2\,H_2O$$

A. 0.093 g Ag_2S

B. 0.370 g Ag_2S

C. 0.185 g Ag_2S

D. 0.105 g Ag_2S

Written Response

Use the following information to answer the next question.

Aluminum chloride can be produced from the reaction of aluminum and chlorine according to the equation:

$$2\,Al + 3\,Cl_2 \rightarrow 2\,AlCl_3$$

1. What is the limiting reagent if 10.0 g of Al react with 15.0 g of chlorine and what mass of $AlCl_3$ could theoretically be produced?

Atomic Theory

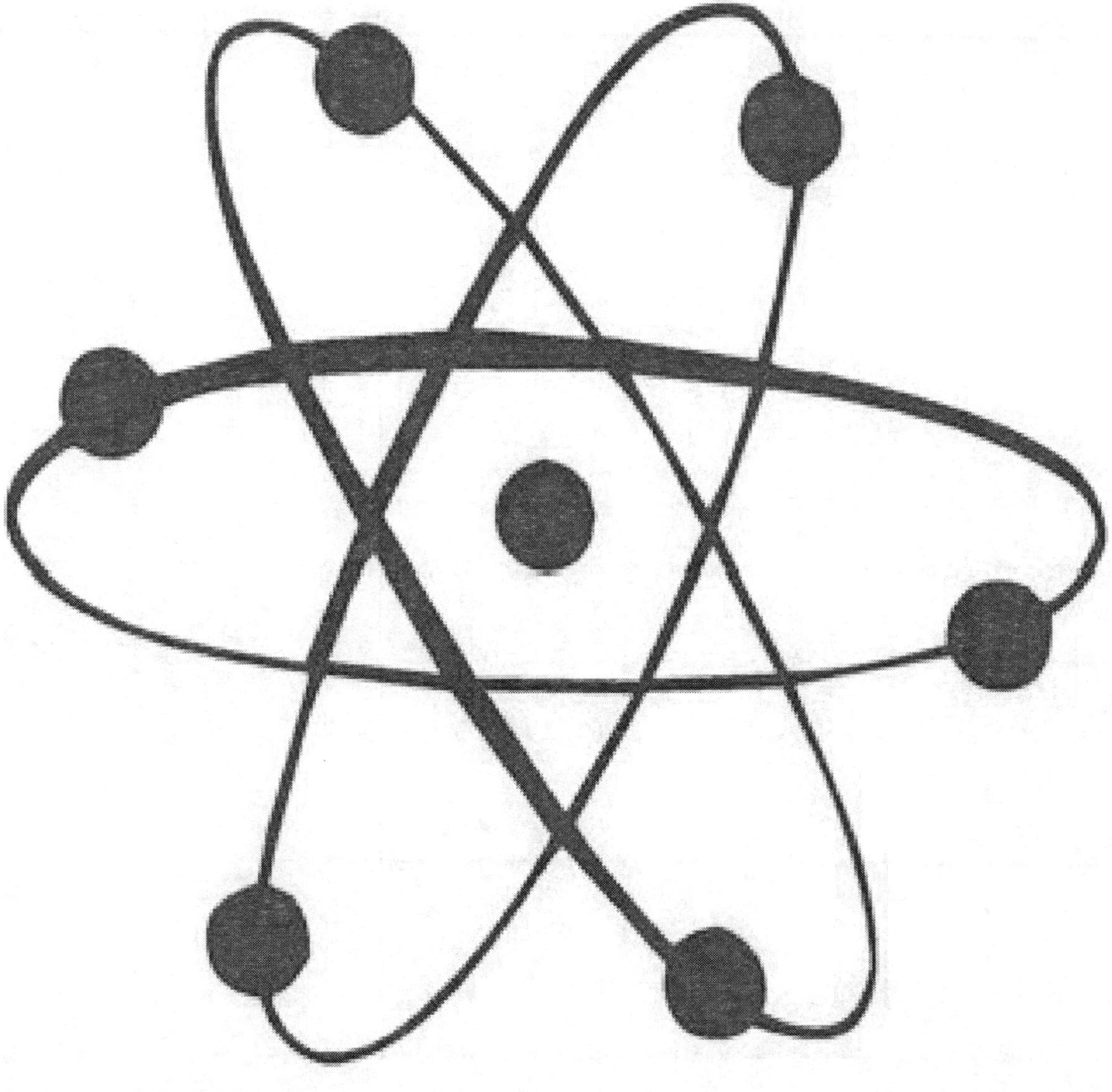

ATOMIC THEORY

Table of Correlations		
Outcomes		Questions
Students are expected to:		
Introduction	5.1.1 describe early models of the atom	1
	5.1.2 describe the relative position, mass, and charge for a proton, neutron, and electron	2, 15, 20
	5.1.3 identify the atomic number for an element, using a table	
	5.1.4 calculate the number of protons and electrons in an atom or ion	3, 4, 5, 6, 7, 12, 13, 18
	5.1.5 define isotope and explain it in terms of atomic structure	8, 16
	5.1.6 calculate the number of neutrons, protons, and electrons for an atom or ion of an isotope given the mass number of the isotope and the charge of the ion	9, 14, 19
	5.1.7 calculate the average atomic mass from isotopic data	
	5.1.8 describe a simple electron arrangement for the first 20 elements	10, 11, 17, 21
Periodic Table	5.2.1 classify elements as metal, non-metal, or metalloid and locate them on the periodic table	26
	5.2.2 describe the similarities and trends among elements using such properties as: melting point, ionization energy, atomic radius, chemical reactivity, ion charge, conductivity	22, 23, 27, 28, WR1
	5.2.3 distinguish the ordering of elements in early periodic tables (based on atomic mass) from the ordering of elements in the modern periodic table (based on atomic number)	NR1
	5.2.4 identify the following families of elements: alkali metals, alkaline earth metals, halogens, noble gases	
	5.2.5 describe some properties of the alkali metals, alkaline earth metals, halogens, and noble gases	
	5.2.6 relate noble gas stability to electron arrangement within the atom	
	5.2.7 predict the probable electron gain or loss for elements in columns 1, 2, 13, 15, 16, and 17 to attain stability	24
	5.2.8 relate the observed charge of monatomic ions of metals and non-metals to numbers of electrons lost or gained	25
	5.2.9 predict the characteristics of elements knowing the characteristics of another element in that family	
	5.2.10 predict the metallic character of an element based upon its position in the table	
Chemical Bonding	5.3.1 define covalent and ionic bonding	29, 30, 35
	5.3.2 define valence electrons	
	5.3.3 demonstrate a knowledge that bonding involves valence electrons	31, 34, 36
	5.3.4 draw an electron dot diagram for an atom	32
	5.3.5 identify from a chemical formula the probable type of bond (ionic or covalent)	33
	5.3.6 draw electron dot diagrams and structural formulae for simple molecules and ions and deduce molecular formulae	

ATOMIC THEORY

INTRODUCTION

5.1.1 Describe early models of the atom

5.1.2 Describe the relative position, mass, and charge for a proton, neutron, and electron

5.1.3 Identify the atomic number for an element, using a table

5.1.4 Calculate the number of protons and electrons in an atom or ion

All matter consists of atoms and all atoms consist of three subatomic particles; electrons, protons and neutrons. All the protons are exactly the same and have a positive electrical charge. The neutrons are all the same and are very slightly greater on mass than the protons. Again all the electrons are identical and have a negative electrical charge. Electrons are much smaller than the other subatomic particles being about 1/1836 the size of a proton.

Mass		
Particle	**grams**	**amu**
Electron	9.109390×10^{-28}	5.485799×10^{-4}
Proton	1.672623×10^{-24}	1.007276
Neutron	1.674929×10^{-24}	1.008644

amu is the atomic mass unit and is used for calculations involving atomic masses as the gram is much too large for convenience. 1 amu = 1/12 of the mass of an atom of 12–C.

The nucleus is the center of the atom and consists of protons and the neutrons. The nucleus has a positive electrical charge due to the presence of the protons. The electrons are arranged on the outside of the nucleus in electron orbitals that are in different shapes at different distances out from the nucleus depending on how much energy they possess. The electrons occupy a relatively vast space given their size so most of the atom is actually empty space. Rutherford demonstrated this with his gold foil experiment. To visualize the atom think of a small pea being the nucleus in the center of your classroom. The entire class would comprise the space where the electrons orbit. It is easy to understand then that the atom is mostly empty space with a positively charged nucleus in the middle of a negatively charged space. The positive charge of the nucleus holds the negatively charged electrons in orbit about the nucleus.

The Periodic Table of Elements contains information about the make up of the various atoms of the elements.

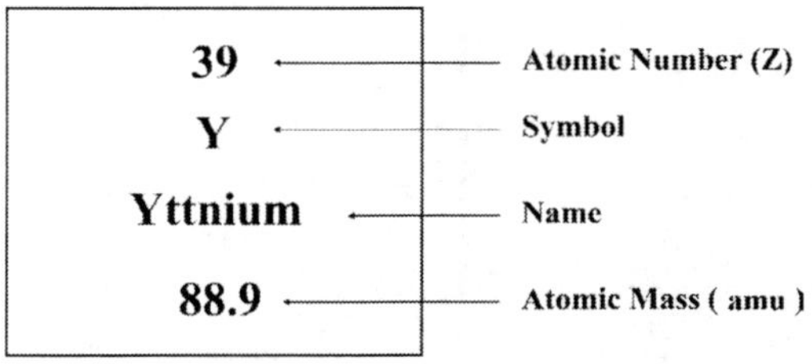

$$\left.\begin{matrix} AtomicMass \rightarrow 88.9 \\ AtomicNumber \rightarrow 39 \end{matrix} Y \right\}$$ This however is how it is written when not on a Periodic Table.

The atomic number is equal to the number of protons in the nucleus of the element. This value never changes in an element. If a proton is added or removed then the atom becomes a different element. The atomic number will also indicate the number of electrons in a neutral atom of an element. Neutral being the number of protons equals the number of electrons. Should the atom gain or lose an electron it becomes an ion and is a charged particle.

Example 1

O^{2-} this is an oxygen ion, oxide, and has a negative charge of 2. The 2^- means that there are two more electrons than protons present about the atom. To determine the number of electrons present just add 2 to the atomic number, the number of protons.

Oxygen is atomic number 8 therefore, the electrons present are 8 + 2 = 10.

Example 2

Cr^{3+} this is a chromium ion with a positive charge of + 3. The positive charge means there are three more protons than electrons. Given that the number of protons does not change ever the atom must have lost three electrons.

Chromium is atomic number 24, therefore electrons present are 24 – 3 = 21.

Related Questions: 1-7, 12, 13, 15, 18, 20

5.1.5 Define isotope and explain it in terms of atomic structure

Atoms with an identical atomic numbers but a different mass numbers are isotopes. The atoms of an element will never vary in the number of protons they have but can vary in the number of neutrons they have. When there is a variation in the number of neutrons there will of course be a difference in atomic mass. To illustrate this we can look at Hydrogen. The majority of hydrogen atoms have one proton and no neutrons there are however two other hydrogen isotopes: Deuterium that has one proton and one neutron and then Tritium that has one proton and two neutrons.

$^{1}_{1}H$	$^{2}_{1}H$	$^{3}_{1}H$
Hydrogen	Deuterium	Tritium

Related Questions: 8, 16

5.1.6 Calculate the number of neutrons, protons, and electrons for an atom or ion of an isotope given the mass number of the isotope and the charge of the ion

The atomic mass is essentially equal to the sum of the masses of protons and neutrons as the mass of the electrons is relatively insignificant. The masses of the protons and neutrons can be considered to be 1 for our purposes in Chemistry 11.Therefore:

Atomic mass = number of protons + number of neutrons

Or

Atomic mass = atomic number + number of neutrons

From this we can determine the number of neutrons:

Number neutrons = atomic mass – number of protons (atomic number)

Example 1

Determine the number of protons, neutrons and electrons in $^{69}_{31}Ga$

The atomic number is 31 therefore the number of protons is 31. The atom has no charge so the number of electrons must equal the number of protons, 31.

Number of neutrons = atomic mass – atomic number

Number of neutrons = 69 – 31 = 38

Example 2

Determine the number of protons, neutrons and electrons in $^{52}_{24}Cr^{+3}$.

The atomic number is 24 therefore the number of protons is 24.

Number of neutrons = atomic mass – atomic number

Number of neutrons = 52 – 24 = 28

This ion has a charge of +3 indicating that it has three more protons than electrons. The number of electrons is then 24 – 3 = 21.

Related Questions: 9, 14, 19

5.1.7 Calculate the average atomic mass from isotopic data

Most elements appear as mixtures of different isotopes in nature. An elements atomic mass as it appears on the periodic table is a weighted average of the naturally occurring isotopic masses of the elements isotopes. The calculation for the average atomic mass is as follows:

Atomic mass = (fraction of isotope) (mass of isotope) + (fraction of isotope)(mass of isotope) + …

It is done for as many isotopes as exists.

Example

Chlorine has two naturally occurring isotopes: 35-Cl with an abundance of 75.77% and a mass of
34.969 amu and 37-Cl with an abundance of 24.23% and a mass of 36.966% amu.

Atomic mass Cl = (fraction 35-Cl)(mass 35 - Cl) + (fraction 37-Cl)(mass 37-Cl)

Atomic mass Cl = (0.7577) (34.969 amu) + (0.2423)(36.966 amu)

Atomic mass Cl = 35.45 amu

5.1.8 Describe a simple electron arrangement for the first 20 elements

It is generally understood that the electrons of an atom orbit about the nucleus and it is the electrostatic attraction of the negative electrons to the positive protons that holds them in this orbit. In reality this is a somewhat more complicated arrangement. There are varying orbits which extend out from the nucleus. These orbits require differing amounts of energy from the electron before it will enter them. Generally the greater the amount of energy the further the orbit (or energy level) is from the nucleus.

The principle quantum number (n) represents the orbits or energy levels. Orbits are also referred to as shells by spectroscopists. These orbits, or shells, contain subshells which describe where the electron may be at any given time. The subshells are referred to here as s, p, d and f. The subshells have orbitals which we will simply say are possible positions for pairs of electrons. As the value of n increases the number of allowed orbitals increases and their size becomes larger thus allowing the electrons to be further from the nucleus.

Please keep in mind that this is a simplified version of atomic orbital theory.

Subshell

s type has 1s orbital and can hold 2 electrons
p type has 3p orbitals and can hold 6 electrons
d type has 5d orbitals and can hold 10 electrons
f type has 7f orbitals and can hold 14 electrons

Orbit 1 has only s
Orbit 2 has s and p
Orbit 3 has s, p and d
Orbit 4 and up has s, p, d, and f

Each subshell in an orbit has a requisite amount of energy required for an electron to fill it. Electrons will fill the orbitals with the lowest energy requirements first unless they are excited by energy added to the system.

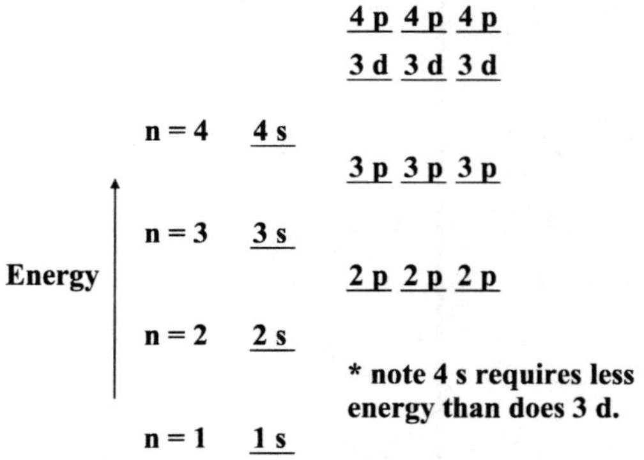

1s or … | ⇐ represents on electron pair. Each orbital can hold 2 electrons that spin about the nucleus in opposite directions.

Order of electron filling

1s → 2s → 2p → 3s → 3p → 4s → 3d → 4p → 5s → 4d → 5p → 6s → 4f … this continues but is beyond the requirements of Chemistry 11.

Writing electronic configurations

These are electronic configurations for elements in their ground state meaning lowest energy state. Electronic configurations show which orbits and subshells have electrons and how many are present in each. They can show relative reactivity of the elements and can be used to predict possible charge on the element if it becomes an ion.

Simply determine the number of the electrons the atom has and place them in the orbits/orbitals per the above order of increasing energy.

Hydrogen has 1 electron → $1s^1$ this means orbit 1, s subshell with 1 electron.

Lithium has 3 electrons → $1s^2\ 2s^1$ this means orbit 1 has its s orbital full with 2 electrons and has 1 electron in its 2nd s orbital.

Carbon has 6 electrons → $1s^2\ 2s^2\ 2p^2$

These can also be expressed showing the electron spins and their placement.

H 1s ↑

Li 1s ↑↓ **2s** ↑

C 1s ↑↓ **2s** ↑↓ **2p** ↑ ↑ _

Manganese has 25 electrons
→ $1s^2\ 2s^2\ 2p^6\ 3s^2\ 3p^6\ 4s^2\ 3d^5$

Related Questions: 10, 11, 17, 21

PERIODIC TABLE

5.2.1 Classify elements as metal, non-metal or metalloid and locate them on the periodic table

5.2.2 Describe the similarities and trends among elements using such properties as: melting point, ionization energy, atomic radius, chemical reactivity, ion charge and conductivity

5.2.3 Distinguish the ordering of elements in early periodic tables (based on atomic mass) from the ordering of elements in the modern Periodic Table (based on atomic number)

5.2.4 Identify the following families of elements: alkali metals, alkaline earth metals, halogens and noble gases

5.2.5 Describe some properties of the alkali metals, alkaline earth metals, halogens and noble gases

5.2.6 Relate noble gas stability to electron arrangement within the atom

5.2.7 Predict the probable electron gain or loss for elements in columns 1,2,13,15,16 and 17 to attain stability

5.2.8 Relate the observed charge of monoatomic ions of metals and non-metals to numbers of electrons lost or gained

5.2.9 Predict the characteristics of elements knowing the characteristics of another element in that family

5.2.10 Predict the metallic character of an element based upon its position in the table

The modern Periodic Table is organized by columns (groups) and rows (periods). The groups run vertically and the periods run horizontally. The arrangement of the elements is not random and reflects the "periodic law" which states that the properties of chemical elements recur periodically when the elements are arranged from lowest to highest atomic numbers. The result is that elements of similar reactivity and with similar properties are all arranged in groups or columns. Recall that the elements of the groups all end with a similar electron configuration which accounts for the similar reactivity.

The major divisions of the periodic table are shown below with a few of their properties.

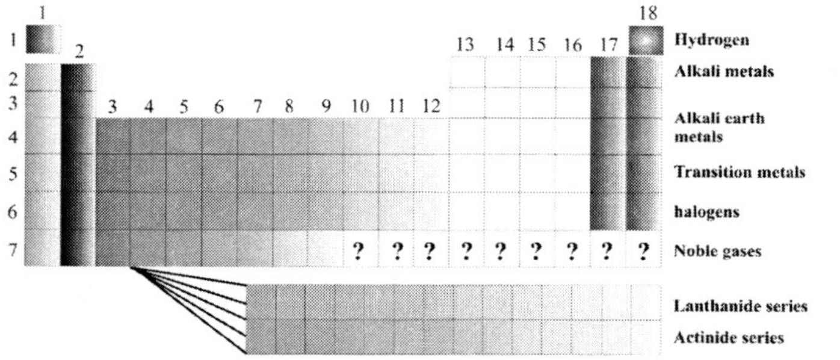

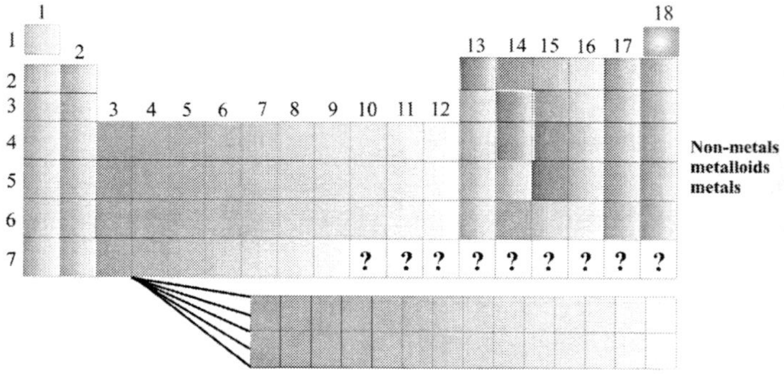

The periodic trends of the elements are shown below.

As you move across from left to right	
Atomic radius	Decreases
Metallic character	Decreases
Electro negativity	Increases
Ionization energy	Increases
reactivity	Decreases

As you move up a group	
Atomic radius	Decreases
Metallic character	Decreases
Electro negativity	Increases
Ionization energy	Increases
reactivity	Decreases

The atoms of the elements are reactive based upon their number of valence electrons. The valence electrons are the electrons found in the s and p subshells. The valence electrons that matter to the reactivity of the atom for our purposes are those electrons in the outer most orbits s and p subshells. The atom is most stable when it has a full valence thus no unfilled s and p orbitals. The noble gases are non-reactive as they have full valences. Atoms will tend to lose and gain electrons in order to become stable – have a full valence.

The column (group) number on the periodic table indicates the number of electrons in the outer orbit of the atom. Columns 1 and 2 have electronic configurations ending in the s subshell. Columns 3 through 12 have electrons ending in the d subshell while columns 13 through 18 have electronic configurations ending in the p subshell. As it is the s and p valance electrons that concern us we will only discuss columns 1, 2, 13, 15-17. The number of valence electrons in the metals tends to be low while the numbers of valence electrons in the non-metals tends to be high. The metals will typically donate electrons and the non-metals will typically accept electrons into their respective valences. Their tendency will to donate accept electrons to obtain the electronic configuration of the noble gas closest in electron number to them and thus be chemically stable.

Elements that donate electrons will have more protons than electrons and will subsequently have a positive charge. Elements that accept electrons into their valence will have more electrons than protons and will subsequently have a negative charge. If we know the column of the element, we can predict its charge based upon the number of electrons it will donate or accept to become chemically stable.

Column number	Tendency	Predicted Charge
1	lose 1 electron	+1
2	lose 2 electrons	+2
13	lose 3 electrons	+3
15	gain 3 electrons	–3
16	gain 2 electrons	–2
17	gain 1 electron	–1

The numbers of valence electrons are same for all elements in any given column and the valence electrons determine how the atoms of the element will react chemically. Knowing this we can say that the elements in a column, family, all have similar chemical reactivity.

Related Questions: 22-28, , WR1, NR1

CHEMICAL BONDING

5.3.1 Define covalent and ionic bonding

5.3.2 Define valence electrons

5.3.3 Demonstrate a knowledge that bonding involves valence electrons

5.3.4 Draw an electron dot diagram for an atom

5.3.5 Identify from a chemical formula the probable type of chemical bond

5.3.6 Draw electron dot diagrams and structural formulae for simple molecules and ions and deduce molecular formulae

Chemical bonds are the results of interactions between valence electrons of atoms. The resulting effects of the interactions hold the atoms within a molecule together.

Typically metals interacting with a non-metal will form an ionic bond. The metal is donating electron(s) and the non-metal is accepting electron(s) resulting in positive and negative charges which hold the resulting ions together. The metal which donates the valence electrons becomes a positive ion and the non-metal which accepts the electrons becomes a negative ion. It is important to note that no two compounds will be equally ionic as there are varying degrees of electron transfer between the atoms. An extremely ionic bond has the electron completely transferred from one atom to the other but there are many ionic bonds which are "partial" as the electron is only partially transferred to from one atom to the other. It all depends on the reactivity of the atoms in question.

Covalent bonds are the result of atoms sharing a pair of electrons so that both of the atoms have some degree of "control" over the electrons. A true covalent bond has the atoms share the pair of electrons equally and this can only occur between two atoms that are identical – of the same element. The sharing is not equal in a compound having covalent bonds. One of the atoms tends to have more control over the electron pair than the other forming a polar – covalent bond which we will still consider a covalent bond type.

The transfer of an electron from one atom to another or the unequal sharing of a pair of electrons is controlled by electronegativity. Linus Pauling defined electronegativity as "the power of an atom in a molecule to attract electrons to itself". The larger the value of the atom's electronegativity, the greater its ability to attract electrons to itself. It is the difference in the electronegativities between bonding atoms that determines the bond type.

Covalent bond electronegativity difference = 0.0–0.2
Polar covalent bond electronegativity difference = 0.2–1.7
Ionic bond electronegativity difference > 1.7

Very basically ionic and very polar covalent bonds form between metals and non-metals while weakly polar covalent and covalent bonds form between non-metals.

We can represent the bonding between atoms of some elements by using electron or Lewis dot diagrams. These diagrams are written showing the valence electrons about the atom and indicate the "pairing" of the bonding valence electrons between the atoms.

Simple Ionic compounds

- draw each atom with its valence electrons
- withdraw lone electrons from the metal to pair up with lone electrons of the non-metal and indicate charges produced

Example

NaCl

Sodium has one valence electron while Chlorine has seven valence electrons.

$$\text{Na}\cdot\quad \cdot\underset{\cdot\cdot}{\overset{\cdot\cdot}{\text{Cl}}}: \;\rightarrow\; \text{Na}^{+}\ :\underset{\cdot\cdot}{\overset{\cdot\cdot}{\text{Cl}}}:$$

Lewis or electron dot diagrams

The octet rules states that most atoms will tend to have eight valence electrons about them. The exception to this is Hydrogen which only has a 1s susbshell and can only hold two valence electrons. To draw the diagram arrange the atoms symmetrically about the central atom(s) and put their valence electrons about them. Pair up the lone "bonding" electrons and redraw showing the paired up electrons as lines representing bonds.

Example

H_2O

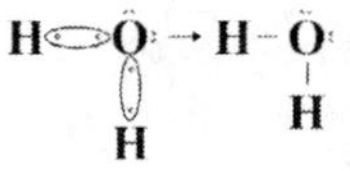

Example

SCl_2

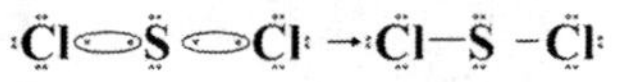

Example

N_2

Example

CH_2O

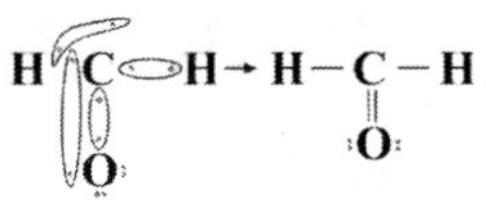

Rules for Ions and more complicated compounds

i) Count up the total number of valence electrons of the atoms of the substance in question. Add one for each negative charge and subtract one for each positive charge if the substance is an ion.

ii) Put 2 electrons between each substance to form the bond.

iii) Fill the octet of the outer atoms, except hydrogen, and put the remaining electrons in pairs about the central atom.

iv) If the central atom does not have the requisite 8 then assign a nonbonding pair about an outer atom to become a bond between it and the central atom.

v) If the substance is an ion put square brackets about the diagram and indicate charge.

Example

CO_3^{-2}

C O −2

$4 + (3\times6) + 2$ = 24 valence electrons

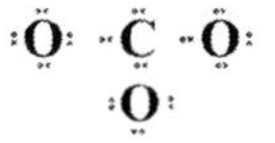

Carbon only has 6 electrons about it so one pair in an oxygen will become a bond

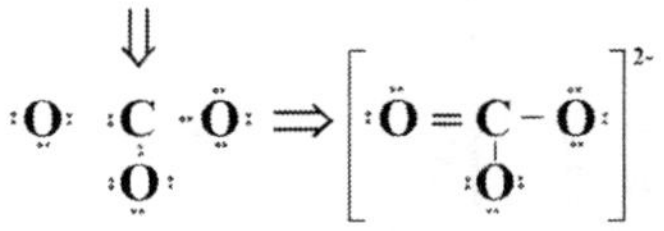

Example

SO_2

S O

$6 + (2\times6)$ = 18 valence electrons

As S is short 2 electrons to have the octet

Related Questions: 29-36

1. Who first determined that an atom contained negatively charged particles?

A. Bohr
B. Spray
C. Thomson
D. Rutherford

2. Who determined that electrons were restricted to specific orbits about the nucleus?

A. Bohr
B. Bond
C. Becquerel
D. Rutherford

3. The number of protons found in a Fe nucleus is

A. 32
B. 28
C. 26
D. 24

4. The number of electrons in orbit about a Cl atom is

A. 17
B. 18.5
C. 19
D. 35.5

5. The number of neutrons in a Mn nucleus is

A. 79.9
B. 30
C. 29.9
D. 25

Mg = 25 protons
Neutrons = (atomic mass) − (atomic #)
= 54.9 − 25
= 29.9

6. The number of electrons in orbit about an F^- ion is

A. 8
B. 9
C. 10
D. 20

7. The number of protons found in a Y^{2+} nucleus is

A. 37
B. 39
C. 41
D. 88.9

8. Isotopes differ in mass due to different numbers of

A. electrons
B. protons
C. neutrons
D. quarks

CHALLENGER QUESTION

9. The following isotopes are found in nature:
^{10}B = 18.9% and ^{11}B = 81.1%
Determine the average atomic mass

A. 10.41
B. 10.5
C. 10.81
D. 11.0

= (% B-10)(mass B-10) + (% B-11)(mass B-11)
= (0.189)(10) + (0.811)(11)
= 10.81

10. What is the electronic configuration of Al?

A. $1s^2 2s^2 2p^6 3s^2 3p^1$
B. $1s^2 2s^2 2p^6 3s^1 3p^2$
C. $1s^2 2s^2 2p^6 3s^2 3p^3$
D. $1s^2 2s^2 2p^6 3s^2 3p^6$

11. What is the electronic configuration of O^{2-}?

A. $1s^2 2s^2 2p^2$
B. $1s^2 2s^2 2p^4$
C. $1s^2 2s^2 2p^6$
D. $1s^2 2s^2 2p^8$

12. The number of protons in As^{3-} is

A. 33
B. 30
C. 36
D. 15

13. The number of protons, electrons and neutrons in Rh^{+2} is

A. 45 protons, 43 electrons, 58 neutrons
B. 45 protons, 45 electrons, 58 neutrons
C. 45 protons, 47 electrons, 58 neutrons
D. 43 protons, 45 electrons, 58 neutrons

P = 45
E = 43
N = atomic mass − # protons
= 58

14. The relative atomic mass of the element Chlorine is 35.453 and there are two naturally occurring isotopes, ^{35}Cl and ^{37}Cl. Which of the following statements would best describe the relative abundance of the isotopes of Chlorine?

A. The isotope ^{35}Cl is about 3 times as abundant as ^{37}Cl.

B. The isotope ^{37}Cl is about 3 times as abundant as ^{35}Cl.

C. The isotopes ^{35}Cl and ^{37}Cl ^{37}Cl are in equal abundance.

D. The isotope ^{35}Cl is about 3 times as abundant as ^{38}Cl.

15. Which statement best compares a neutron and a proton?

A. Their charges are different and their masses are similar.

B. Their charges are opposite and their masses are similar.

C. Their charges are similar and their masses are different.

D. Their charges are similar and their masses are similar.

16. Consider two atoms that have slightly different masses. They could be isotopes of the same element if they have the same

A. number of protons but different numbers of neutrons.

B. number of neutrons but different numbers of protons.

C. number of protons and the same number of neutrons.

D. number of electrons but different number of protons.

17. The electronic configuration of Si is

A. $1s^2 2s^2 2p^6 3s^2 3p^2$

B. $1s^2 2s^2 2p^6 3s^2 p^2$

C. $1s^2 2s^2 2p^6 3s^1 3p^2$

D. $1s^2 2s^2 2p^6 3s^2 3p^3$

Use the following information to answer the next question.

By mass, approximately 10% of the human body is made up of hydrogen and 65% is comprised of oxygen.

18. Hydrogen has an atomic number of 1 whereas oxygen has an atomic number of 8 because each hydrogen atom has

A. one energy level whereas each oxygen atom has eight energy levels

B. one proton whereas each oxygen atom has eight protons

C. one neutron whereas each oxygen atom has eight neutrons

D. an atomic mass of one, whereas each oxygen atom an atomic mass of eight

Use the following information to answer the next question.

Carbon-14, unlike carbon-12, is a radioactive isotope of carbon. All organic matter contains a certain amount of carbon-14. After an organism dies, the carbon-14 within it begins to decay at a constant rate. Earth scientists at the University of Alberta use carbon dating to estimate the age of organic material from the last glacial era. Such information enables them to predict the location of natural resources and minerals.

19. A difference between carbon-14 and carbon-12 is that carbon-14 has

A. more protons than does carbon-12
B. a lower ion charge than does carbon-12
C. more neutrons than does carbon-12
D. a higher ion charge than does carbon-12

Use the following information to answer the next question.

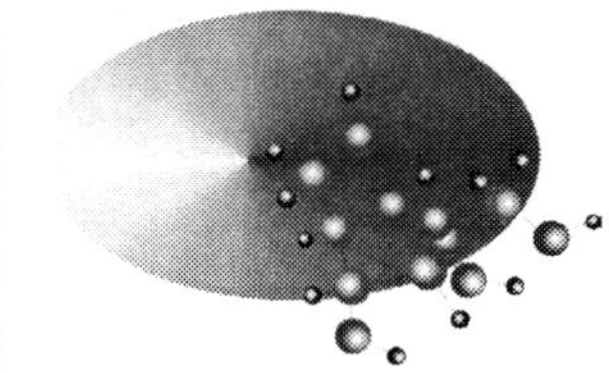

The Scanning Tunnelling Electron Microscope (S.T.E.M.) is a powerful tool that allows scientists to study molecules and atoms. In simple terms, the STEM works by mapping the surface of a material by scanning it for "bumps and dents." Bumps represent atoms, and dents represent the spaces between atoms. The structure of various molecules can be determined using this technique.

20. Which of the following statements regarding the mass of atomic structures is true?

A. Protons and electrons have a larger mass than neutrons.
B. Electrons and neutrons have a larger mass than protons.
C. Neutrons and protons have a larger mass than electrons.
D. Protons, neutrons, and electrons have approximately the same mass.

21. A potassium atom has 19 protons. A potassium atom also has 19 electrons arranged in energy levels in which of the following sequences?

A. 1, 2, 8, 8
B. 2, 8, 8, 1
C. 8, 8, 2, 1
D. 18, 1

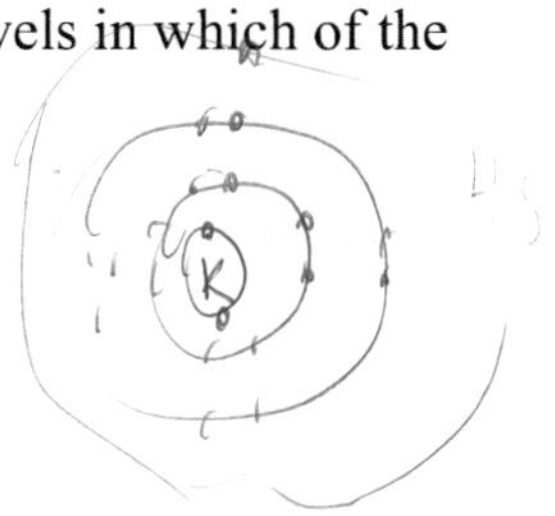

22. Which element has the smallest radius based upon it periodic table position?

A. He
B. Ne
C. Ar
D. Kr

23. Which element has the smallest radius based upon it periodic table position?

A. K
B. Ca
C. Sc
D. Y

24. The ion S^{2-} has its charge because it has

A. lost 2 protons
B. gained 2 protons
C. lost 2 electrons
D. gained 2 electrons

25. Based on valence electrons, what charge would elements in group 15 have?

A. + 3
B. – 1
C. – 2
D. – 3

26. Which of the following is an Actinide element?

A. U
B. Nd
C. Rf
D. Hf

Use a Periodic Table to answer the next two questions.

27. Given that lithium (Li) reacts moderately with water and sodium (Na) reacts vigorously with water, which one of the following metals would be expected to react most vigorously with water?

A. Fe
B. Al
C. Be
D. Cs

Use the following information to answer the next question.

In 1962 at the University of British Columbia Canadian chemist Neil Bartlett synthesized a compound that most chemists thought could never be synthesized because it contained an element that was thought to be non-reactive. Bartlett's synthesis showed that although this element had very low reactivity, it could be reactive under the right circumstances.

28. Based on your knowledge of the relative reactivity of the elements in the periodic table, which of the following compounds did Bartlett most likely synthesize?

A. $RhPtF_6$
B. $KPtF_6$
C. $XePtF_6$
D. $SePtF_6$

Use the following information to answer the next question.

Internal differentiation describes a period in Earth's geological history when heavier elements moved toward Earth's centre, and lighter elements moved toward the surface. As a result of ***internal differentiation***, Earth has a core composed of heavy elements, such as iron and nickel, and an atmosphere composed of lighter elements such as nitrogen and oxygen.

A. Sulfur
B. Zinc
C. Neon
D. Gold
E. Iron
F. Sodium
G. Helium

Numerical Response

CHALLENGER QUESTION

1. The relative location of the seven elements shown above are represented in the diagram. According to the theory of *internal differentiation*, which regions could represent helium, iron, and sodium, respectively?

1, 5, 3

29. A chemical bond can be described as

A. a shared pair of electrons
B. orbital electrons
C. a transfer of an electron pair
D. unequal use of two electrons

30. An ionic bond is

A. an equal sharing of an electron pair
B. the attraction between positive and negative ions
C. a metal and a non-metal joining together
D. the attraction between positive ions

31. What type of bonding involves an electron transfer?

A. ionic bonds
B. London bonds
C. covalent bonds
D. polar covalent bonds

32. What type of bond is present in CF_4?

A. ionic **B.** double
C. covalent **D.** hydrogen

33. Which is the correct Lewis dot diagram for H_2CO?

A.
H
|
C = Ö (with lone pairs)
|
H

B. H–C̈ = Ö–H

C.
H
|
C = Ö: (with lone pairs)
|
H

D. H–C ≡ O–H

34. Which of the following has 2 lone pairs of electrons and 2 bonding electrons?

A. Iron **B.** Sulphur
C. Chlorine **D.** Phosphorus

35. Chemical bonds form in order to

A. transfer electron to the inner orbits
B. transfer lone electron pairs to bonds
C. have the outer orbits release electrons
D. have electrons obtain a stable configuration

36. When the atoms of Carbon and Sulphur come together to produce the compound CS_2, the bonding electrons

A. are shared and ionic bonds are formed
B. are shared and covalent bonds are formed
C. are transferred and ionic bonds are formed
D. are transferred and hydrogen bonds are formed

Written Response

1. Use the following compounds and your knowledge of the Periodic Table to determine the probable formula for a Hydride of Sulphur.

$KH, CaH_2, Ga_2H_6, AsH_3, H_2Se, HBr$

NOTES

any PACE, any PLACE, any TIME
Quality Educational Choices With Christian Values
WWW.BCONLINESCHOOL.CA
Sign up for summer or fall High School online courses written from a Christian worldview that meet BC graduation requirements.
Work with experienced certified teachers in an interactive, communicative online setting.
No cost for current Grade 10-12 students.
Online Courses Available
Check our website for information on Advanced Placement courses and much more...
Applications of Math 10
Bible 10
English 10
Essentials of Math 10
Physical Education 10
Planning 10
Principles of Math 10
Science 10
Social Studies 10
Accounting 11
Applications of Math 11
Biology 11
Business Applications 11
Chemistry 11
Christian Studies 11
Communications 11
English 11
Essentials of Math 11
Marketing 11
Physics 11
Principles of Math 11
Science & Technology 11
French 11
Social Studies 11
Studio Arts 11/12
Applications of Math 12
Biology 12
Chemistry 12
Christian Studies 12
Communications 12
Comparitive Civ. 12
English 12
English Literature 12
Entrepreneurship 12
Geography 12
History 12
Journalism 12
Law 12
Physics 12
Principles of Math 12
Online Graduation Portfolio
BC Online School
WWW.BCONLINESCHOOL.CA

Solution Chemistry

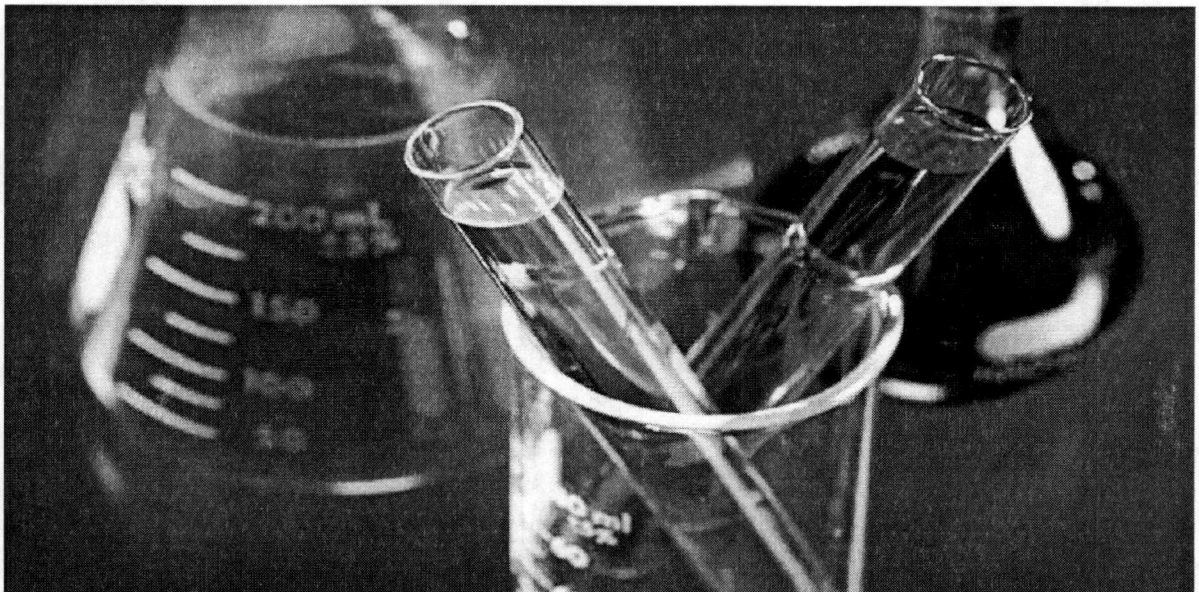

SOLUTION CHEMISTRY

Table of Correlations		
Outcomes		**Questions**
Students are expected to:		
Introduction	6.1.1 define a solution as a homogeneous mixture	1
	6.1.2 classify a solution as a system distinct from a pure solid, liquid, or gas	2, 10
	6.1.3 identify the solute and the solvent as the components of a solution	
	6.1.4 describe the causes of molecular polarity	3, 8
	6.1.5 categorize various common solvents as polar and non-polar	
	6.1.6 on the basis of observations, make deductions concerning the solubility of polar and non-polar solutes in polar and non-polar solvents	4
	6.1.7 use lab observations to describe the relative conductivity of several solutes in aqueous solution	
	6.1.8 summarize the results of a conductivity experiment as to the types of solute that conduct electricity when dissolved in water	5, 9 7
	6.1.9 propose a mechanism that explains the conductivity of soluble salts in water	
	6.1.10 write dissociation or ionization equations for several substances that dissolve to give conducting solutions	6, WR1
	6.1.11 calculate the molarity of each ion in a salt solution given the molarity of the solution	
	6.1.12 calculate the concentration of ions resulting when two solutions of known concentration and volume are mixed (assuming no reaction)	

SOLUTION CHEMISTRY

INTRODUCTION

6.1.1 Define solution as a homogenous mixture

6.1.2 Classify a solution as a system distinct from a pure solid, liquid or gas

6.1.3 Identify the solute and solvent as the components of a solution

6.1.4 Describe the causes of molecular polarity

6.1.5 Categorize various solvents as polar and non-polar

6.1.6 On the basis of observations, make deductions concerning the solubility of polar and non-polar solutes in polar and non-polar solvents

6.1.7 Use lab observations to describe the relative conductivity of several solutes in aqueous solution

6.1.8 Summarize the types of solutes that conduct electricity when dissolved in water

6.1.9 Propose a mechanism that explains the conductivity of soluble salts in water

6.1.10 Write dissociation equations for several substances that give conducting solutions

6.1.11 Calculate the molarity of each ion in solution given the molarity of the solution

6.1.12 Calculate the concentration of ions resulting when two solutions of known concentration and volume are mixed (assume no reaction)

Solutions are homogeneous mixtures of pure substances.

Any homogeneous mixture of pure substances is a solution. This would therefore include solutions of solids dissolved in liquids, liquids dissolved in liquids, and gases dissolved in liquids, gases dissolved in gases, and even solids dissolved in solids.
In chemistry, our main focus will be on solutions involving solids dissolved in liquids, and in particular, solids dissolved in water or aqueous solutions. Aqueous solutions are always clear. If an aqueous mixture is cloudy, like milk, it is a suspension, not a solution. The substance which is dissolved is called the solute and the substance which does the dissolving is called the solvent. To clarify, in a salt-water solution, the solute is salt and the solvent is water.

Solutes can also be defined as the portion of a solution in lesser quantity while the solvent can be defined as the portion of the solution in greater quantity.

Molecular Polarity in Solutions

Molecular polarity in solutions affects the dissolving of solutes and how the solutions are formed. The polarity is a result of intermolecular forces termed Van der Waals forces. The two types of Van der Waals forces which have the most significant effect of solutions are dipole-dipole and hydrogen bonding.

Dipole-Dipole forces are the result of polar molecules where the positive dipole of one molecule attracts the negative dipole of another molecule. Dipoles themselves are partial charges resulting from molecules formed on atoms with differing electronegativities. The electrons are only partially withdrawn from one atom to another in this case resulting in a partial positive and partial negative charge.

H — Br

d^+ ↗ dipole positive **d^- ↖ dipole negative**

Electro negative of H is 2.2 while Br is 2.7. The result is the shared electrons are pulled closer to Br and away from H

Hydrogen bonding exists when there are hydrogen atom(s) bonded with highly electronegative atoms such as Oxygen or Nitrogen. These molecules have strong dipoles. The Hydrogen end of the molecules are partially positive and are attracted to the negative portion of other molecules – Oxygen or Nitrogen. This is a polar bonding that holds the molecules together and is the strongest of the Van der Waals forces.

In order for the molecules to have molecular polarity in a solution they must have a dipole and they must be asymmetrical. If they are symmetrical then the dipole interactions are not possible due to positioning.

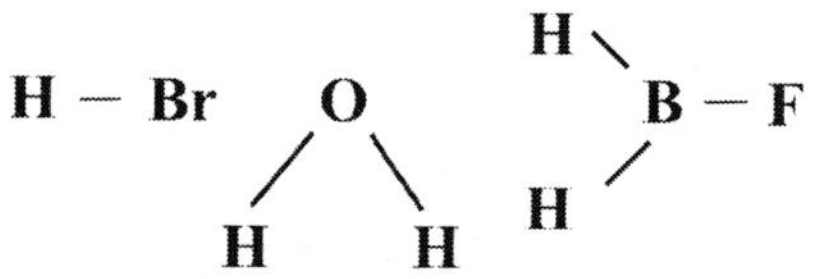

Depending on whether the solvent has molecular polarity or not will determine if it is to be a polar or nonpolar solvent. Polar solvents like water, ethanol and acetone are best at dissolving polar solutes while nonpolar solvents like benzene and carbon tetrachloride are best at dissolving nonpolar solutes. Ionic compounds and those with stronger dipoles will go into solution best with polar solvents as the molecules of the solvent have enough of a polar force to pull the solute molecules apart and allow them to separate into the solvent. Nonpolar solvents do not have enough polar force and cannot pull ionic or polar molecules apart from one another. If the polar molecules cannot be pulled apart from one another they cannot dissolve. Only nonpolar solutes can be pulled apart by the nonpolar solvents and go into solution with them. The rule: LIKE DISSOLVES LIKE.

Conducting Solutions

Electricity is conducted by a flow of electrical charges, so for a solution to be able to conduct an electrical current the solution must contain electrically charged particles. The charged particles in a solution are ions and a solution will conduct if it contains ions. The positively charged ions will travel towards the cathode and the negatively charged particles will travel towards the anion. This flow of electrical charges, the ions in the solution, will complete the circuit and allow the electrical current to flow.

Solutions must contain ions to conduct an electrical current therefore they must have an ionic compound dissolved in the solution. Ionic compounds will dissociate in the solution and exist as the ions that form them providing the negatively and positively charged particle required for conduction. Ionic compounds are typically acids and metal-non-metal compounds. Acids are generally recognized as starting with Hydrogen such as HCl, HI, HNO_3 etc., while ionic compounds are recognized as those that begin with a metal and end with a non-metal such as NaOH, KCl, YNO_3 etc. If a compound begins with a non-metal it is unlikely to form a conducting solution as it is not an ionic compound.

Dissociation Equations and Ion Concentrations

When ionic compounds go into solution the polar forces of the solvent pull the ions of the compound apart and it exists as the ions that form the compound while in the solution. This event is described with a dissociation equation that shows the compound and the ions it forms as it goes into the solution.

Example

$NaCl_{(s)} \rightarrow Na^{+}{}_{(aq)} + Cl^{-}_{(aq)}$ (aq) means in solution with water

Example

$AlCl_{3(s)} \rightarrow Al^{3+}{}_{(aq)} + 3Cl^{-}_{(aq)}$ note there are 3 Cl in $AlCl_3$ therefore there are $3Cl^-$ ions produced in the solution

Let us consider the above equation in terms of quantities. 1 mole of $AlCl_3$ dissociates and forms
1 mole of Al^{+3} ions and 3 moles of Cl^- ions. This principle is used to determine the concentration of ions in a solution of known concentration.

Example

2.5M $AlCl_{3(s)} \rightarrow Al^{3+}_{(aq)} + 3Cl^{-}_{(aq)}$

$[Al^{3+}] = 2.5M$

$[Cl^-] = 3(2.5M) = 7.5M$

Dilutions and Ion Concentrations

These calculations involve determining the new molarities of the solutes and from those determining the ion concentrations as was done above.

Example

Determine the concentration of all ions present when 25.00 mL of 0.100M NaCl is mixed with 15.00 mL of 0.250M $AlCl_3$.

First calculate the molarities of the compounds after the dilution using the dilution formula $M_iV_i = M_fV_f$.

$$\text{Diluted [NaCl]} = \frac{(0.100\,M)(0.02500\,L)}{(0.04000\,L)} = 0.0625\ M\ NaCl$$

$$\text{Diluted } [AlCl_3] = \frac{(0.250\,M)(0.01500\,L)}{(0.040000\,L)} = 0.0938\ M\ AlCl_3$$

Secondly write the dissociation equations for the compounds and from them determine the concentration of the ions.

$$NaCl_{(s)} \rightarrow Na^{+}{}_{(aq)} + Cl^{-}_{(aq)}$$
0.0625M so 0.0625M 0.0625M

$$AlCl_{3(s)} \rightarrow Al^{3+}{}_{(aq)} + 3Cl^{-}_{(aq)}$$
0.0938M so 0.0938M 3(0.0938M)=0.281M

$[Na^{+}] = 0.0625M$

$[Al^{3+}] = 0.0938M$

$[Cl^{-}]$ comes from both compounds so we must sum the concentrations of the Chloride ions. = 0.0625M + 0.281M = 0.344M

Related Questions: 1-10, WR1

1. A solution can be described as

A. a clear suspension
B. a solid and a liquid
C. a homogenous mixture
D. a heterogeneous mixture

2. The component of a solution in greater quantity is the

A. solid
B. solute
C. solvent
D. suspension

3. A polar compound would dissolve best in

A. water
B. turpentine
C. a polar solvent
D. a non-polar solvent

4. What type of solvent will conduct a current?

A. miscible liquid
B. ionic compound
C. covalent compound
D. molecular compound

5. Which of the following is the dissociation equation for $CaCl_2$?

A. $CaCl_{2(s)} \rightarrow Ca^{2+}{}_{(aq)} + 2Cl^{-}{}_{(aq)}$

B. $CaCl_{2(aq)} \rightarrow Ca^{2+}{}_{(aq)} + 2Cl^{-}{}_{(aq)}$

C. $CaCl_{2(s)} \rightarrow Ca^{1+}{}_{(s)} + 2Cl^{-}{}_{(aq)}$

D. $CaCl_{2(s)} \rightarrow Ca^{2+}{}_{(aq)} + Cl^{-}{}_{(aq)}$

CHALLENGER QUESTION

6. For 0.500 M $K_2CO_{3(aq)}$ the concentrations of the ions are

A. $[K^+] = 0.500\,M, [CO_3^{2-}] = 1.00\,M$

B. $[K^+] = 0.500\,M, [CO_3^{2-}] = 0.500\,M$

C. $[K^+] = 1.00\,M, [CO_3^{2-}] = 1.00\,M$

D. $[K^+] = 1.00\,M, [CO_3^{2-}] = 0.500\,M$

CHALLENGER QUESTION

7. What is the molarity of $[Na^+]$ if 10.00mL of 0.100 M NaCl is added to 15.00 mL of 0.200M Li_2CO_3

A. 0.0667 M

B. 0.0400 M

C. 0.00250 M

D. 0.00150 M

8. Which of the following substances would be the most soluble in the nonpolar solvent pentane?

A. AgBr

B. Br_2

C. CsBr

D. $MgBr_2$

9. A conducting solution could be formed by a solution of which compound?

A. KCl

B. CCl_4

C. PF_3

D. SCl_4

10. A solution is formed by mixing propanol and ethanol. The propanol forms 35% of the solution and the ethanol forms 65% of the solution. Which of the following statements best describes this solution?

A. Ethanol is the solvent and propanol is the solute.

B. Propanol is the solvent and ethanol is the solute.

C. Neither is the solvent as only water can be a solvent.

D. Propanol and ethanol both act as solvents.

Written Response

1. Wanda combines two solutions, 125.0mL of a 0.250M K_2SO_4 solution with 175.0mL of 0.450M KI.
Determine the resulting concentration of the Potassium ion in the solution.

Organic Chemistry

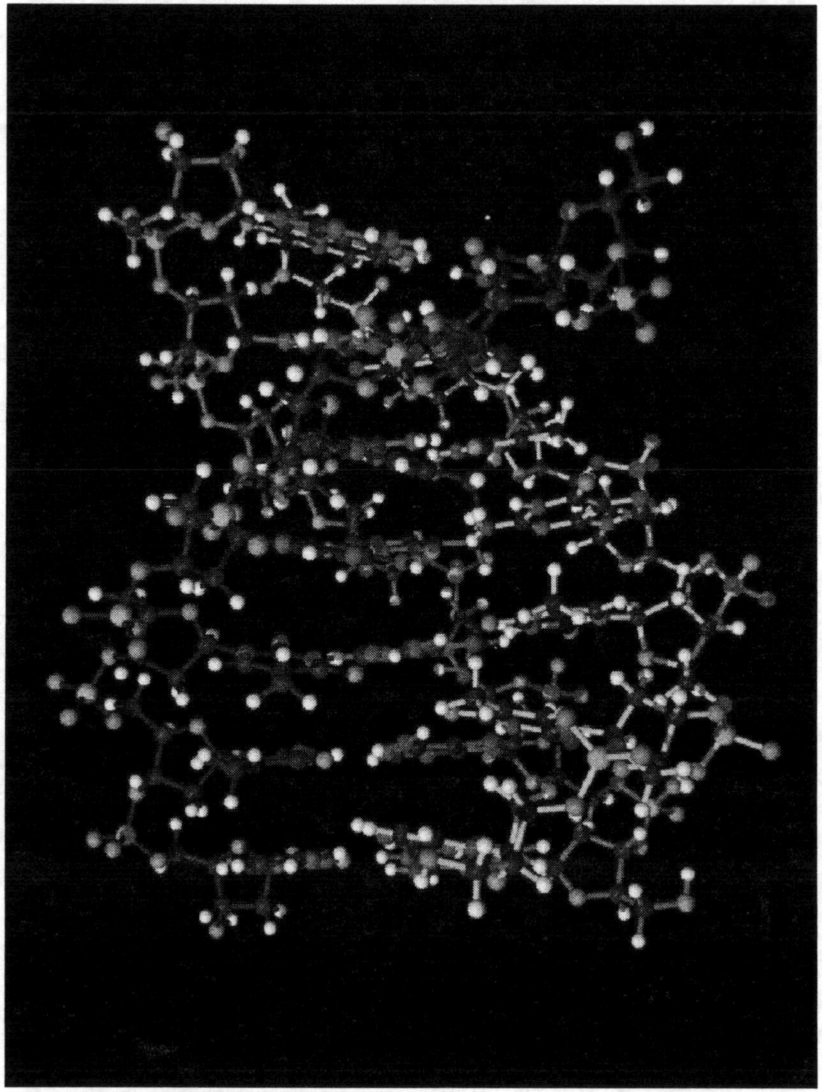

ORGANIC CHEMISTRY

Table of Correlations			
Outcomes			**Questions**
Students are expected to:			
Introduction	7.1.1	identify the multiple bonding character of carbon atoms	
	7.1.2	identify carbon as the "backbone" of organic chemistry	
	7.1.3	relate organic chemistry to products such as plastics, fuels, pharmaceutical drugs, pesticides, insecticides, solvents, synthetics	
	7.1.4	identify major sources of organic compounds	13
	7.1.5	describe a specific industrial application of organic chemistry	
Hydrocarbons	7.2.1	define hydrocarbon, alkane, alkene, alkyne, cyclic, and aromatic as they relate to organic compounds	14, 15
	7.2.2	classify a hydrocarbon as either saturated or unsaturated	1
	7.2.3	compare the geometry of single, double, and triple bonds between two carbon atoms	12
	7.2.4	compare the rotational ability in single, double, and triple bonds	
	7.2.5	name and draw structures of alkanes, alkenes, and alkynes up to C_{10}	2, 3, 8, NR3
	7.2.6	recognize and name the substituent groups methyl, ethyl, fluoro, chloro, bromo, and iodo	
	7.2.7	name and draw structures of simple substituted alkanes up to C_{10}	
	7.2.8	identify cis- or trans-isomers of alkenes	7, 9, 10
	7.2.9	draw a structure of a benzene ring	4
Functional Groups	7.3.1	describe the term functional group and relate it to classes of compounds	
	7.3.2	identify a compound as an alcohol, aldehyde, ketone, ether, organic acid, ester, amine, or amide when given a structural diagram	5, 6, 11, NR2, NR4, NR1
	7.3.3	name and draw structures for simple alcohols	
	7.3.4	describe how an ester can be prepared through the reaction of an alcohol and an organic acid and how it can be detected (by its aroma)	

ORGANIC CHEMISTRY

INTRODUCTION

7.1.1 Identify the multiple bonding character of carbon atoms

7.1.2 Identify carbon as the backbone of organic chemistry

7.1.3 Relate organic chemistry to products such as plastics, fuels, pharmaceutical drugs, pesticides, insecticides, solvents, synthetics

7.1.4 Identify major sources of organic compounds

7.1.5 Describe a specific industrial application of organic chemistry

Organic Chemistry is the branch of chemistry dealing with studies of organic compounds. As the names imply, organic compounds were thought to be the compounds responsible for maintaining and reproducing life while inorganic compounds are the compounds present in minerals.

Today these definitions have broadened to the place where organic compounds are **molecular** compounds of carbon, having covalent bonds within molecules. All other carbon compounds, such as carbonates, bicarbonate, and cyanides are inorganic. Oxides of carbon such as CO and CO_2 are also inorganic, even though they are molecular compounds of carbon.

Carbon is having a special ability to make bonds with itself to form chains. This property is called catenation. The property of catenation serves as a backbone of organic chemistry.

Carbon is also having a special character of forming multiple bonds i.e. forming bonds by using more than one pair of electron. For example,

Single Bond: Ethane

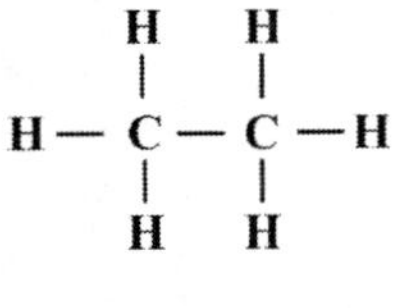

Double Bond: Ethene

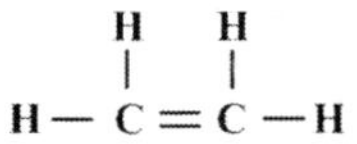

Triple Bond: Ethyne

$H-C\equiv C-H$

Carbon is present in DNA. Fossil fuels such as lignite coal and oil are the major sources of organic compounds. A wide variety of things that we use daily contains carbon-rich organic compounds, for example wool, silk, cotton, nylon, polyester. Organic compounds are also used in various types of plastics, pharmaceutical drugs, solvents and synthetics.

Related Question: 13

HYDROCARBONS

7.2.1 Define hydrocarbons, alkane, alkene, alkyne, cyclic, and aromatic as they relate to organic compounds

7.2.2 Classify a hydrocarbon as either saturated or unsaturated

Hydrocarbons are the compounds that contain only carbon and hydrogen. They are classified as aliphatic or aromatic compounds. Hydrocarbons can be saturated or unsaturated.

Saturated hydrocarbon is an organic compound in which a carbon atom forms a single bond with another atom. For example, C_3H_8, Propane

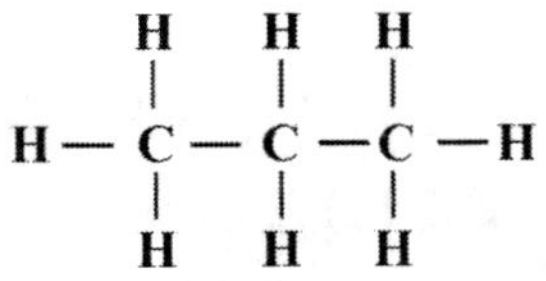

Table 4-1

Aliphatics			
Family Name	General Formula	Recognizable Characteristic	Examples
Alkanes	$C_n H_{2n+2}$	saturated; all single bonds between carbons	2-methylpentane $CH_3-\underset{CH_3}{\underset{\mid}{CH}}-CH_2-CH_2-CH_3$
Alkenes	$C_n H_{2n}$	unsaturated; 1 double bond	2-butene $CH_3-CH=CH-CH_3$
Alkynes	$C_n H_{2n-2}$	unsaturated; 1 triple bond	propyne $CH\equiv C-CH_3$
Cycloalkanes	$C_n H_{2n}$	saturated; ring structure	cyclobutane 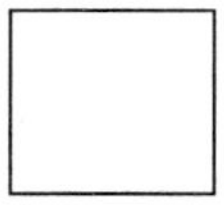
Cycloalkenes	$C_n H_{2n-2}$	1 double bond; ring structure	cyclohexene 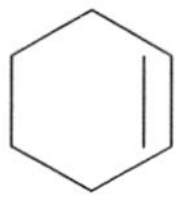
Aromatics			
Aryl	C_6H_6 or $C_6H_{<6}R$	contain benzene, C_6H_6: 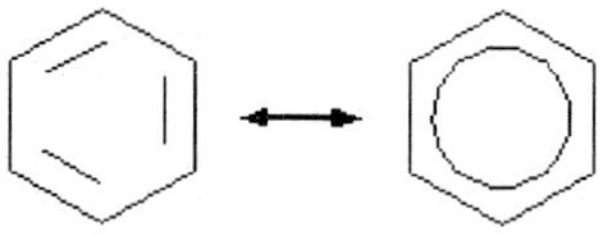	methyl benzene 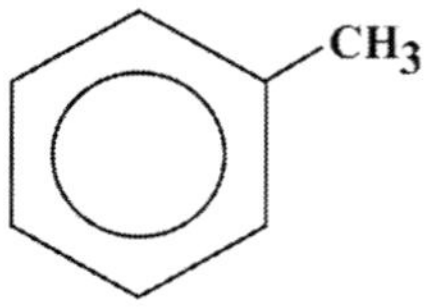

Table 4-2

Family	Functional Group	General Formula	General Name	Example
alcohols	**hydroxyl:** $-O-H$	$R-O-H$	~ anol	CH_3-O-H methanol
aldehydes	**carbonyl:** $-C(=O)-$	$R(H)-C(=O)-H$	~ anal	$CH_3-C(=O)-H$ ethanal
ketones	**carbonyl:** (as above)	$R-C(=O)-R'$	~ none	$CH_3-C(=O)-CH_3$ propanone
carboxylic acids	**carboxyl:** (combination of carbonyl and hydroxyl) $-C(=O)-O-H$	$R(H)-C(=O)-O-H$	~ oic acid	$CH_3-C(=O)-O-H$ ethanoic acid
organic halides	halogen atom:	R-X, where X represents a halogen atom	Halo	$CH_3-CH(Br)-CH_3$ 2-bromopropane
amines	**amine:** (see general formula)	$R-N(R''(H))-R'(H)$ **	~amine	$CH_3-N(H)-H$ methylamine
amides	**amide:** (see general formula)	$R(H)-C(=O)-NH_2$	~ amide	$CH_3-C(=O)-N(H)-H$ ethanamide
esters	**ester:** (see general formula)	$R(H)-C(=O)-O-R'$	~ yl ~ noate	Ethylmethanoate

Unsaturated hydrocarbon is an organic compound in which chain or ring are not completely satisfied with a single bond and hence forms double or triple bonds. The unsaturated are more reactive than saturated compounds. For example, C_2H_4 Ethylene is a double bond,

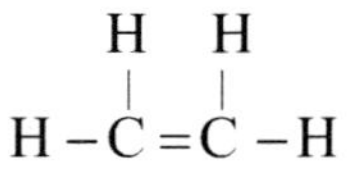

and C_2H_2 Ethyne is a triple bond.

H— C≡C —H

Related Questions: 1, 14, 15

7.2.3 Compare the geometry of single, double, and triple bonds between two carbon atoms

7.2.4 Compare the rotational ability in single, double, and triple bonds

7.2.5 Name and draw structures of alkanes, alkenes, and alkynes up to C_{10}

7.2.6 Recognize and name the substituent groups methyl, ethyl, fluoro, chloro, bromo, and iodo

7.2.7 Name and draw structures of simple substituted alkanes to C_{10}

7.2.8 Identify cis- or trans-isomers of alkenes

7.2.9 Draw a structure of a benzene ring

*Hydrocarbons, at main level C_xH_y, can be divided into the classes as shown in **Table 4-1**. Abbreviated nomenclature rules, with examples, are provided here.*

Number (carbon atom) prefixes

1 *meth*	6 *hex*
2 *eth*	7 *hept*
3 *prop*	8 *oct*
4 *but*	9 *non*
5 *pent*	10 *dec*

Aliphatics

1. Identify the longest continuous chain of carbon atoms (longest continuous chain, containing the double or triple bond, in alk*enes* or alk*ynes*). Write the root name using the number (carbon atom) prefix and the ending *ane*, *ene*, or *yne*, depending on whether it is an alkane, alkene, or alkyne. This will come at the **end** of the name.

2. Number the chain from the end closest to the first branch point (from the end closest to the double or triple bond in alk*enes* or alk*ynes*).

3. The position of the double or triple bond is indicated with a number for alkenes and alkynes.

4. Name branches with the appropriate prefix and a *yl* ending.

5. If there is more than one branch, branches should be listed in *alphabetical order*.

6. Complete the name with branches in alphabetical order, numbers to locate the branches, and the root name. Always have the lowest set of numbers for alkanes. If possible, have the numbers in ascending order.

In the following examples, the long chain is identified with a shaded line.

propane

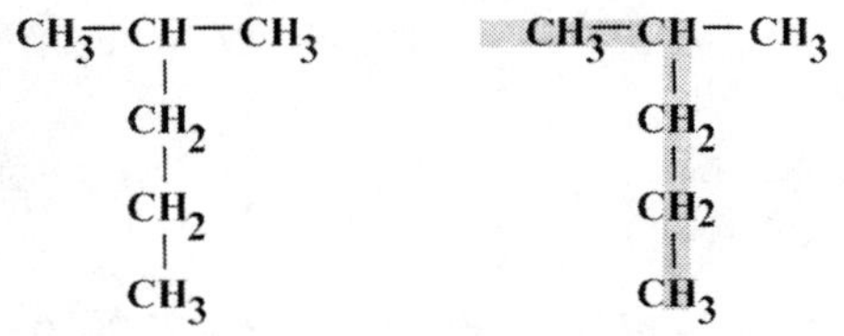

2–methylpentane

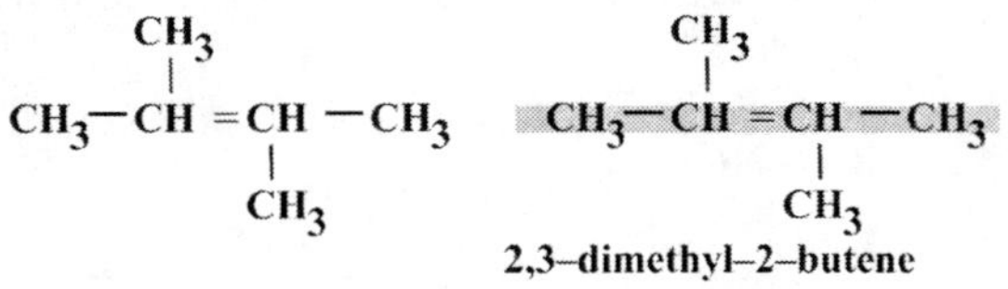

2,3–dimethyl–2–butene

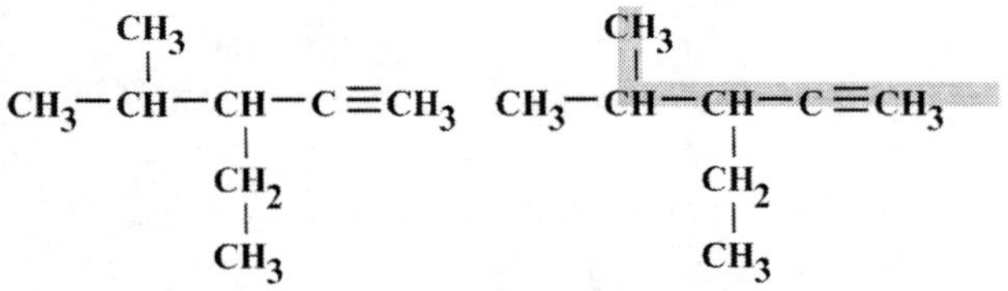

3–ethyl–4–methyl–1–pentyne

[**Note:** In the last example, you could also find the long chain by going straight across.]

Cycloalkanes and Cycloalkenes

These compounds are like alkanes and alkenes except that at one point the chain is joined to itself to form a ring.

To name the compound, count the number of carbon atoms in the ring, give it the alkane or alkene name, and add the prefix *cyclo*.

Examples

Aromatics

Aromatic compounds all contain the compound benzene, C_6H_6.

Benzene is composed of a ring of 6 carbons with delocalized hybrid bonds between carbons. Each carbon could be pictured as bonding to its neighbouring carbon by a bond, which is a cross between a single and a double bond. We draw benzene as , not as , which would be cyclohexane.

Aromatic nomenclature will be shown by example with the following three notes.

1. Disubstituted aromatics may be named using the following prefixes:

   ortho, *o* meaning 1, 2
   meta, *m* meaning 1, 3
   para, *p* meaning 1, 4

2. The lowest set of numbers is the major priority in numbering.

3. The name *phenyl* is used when the benzene ring is labeled as a branch. Examples are:

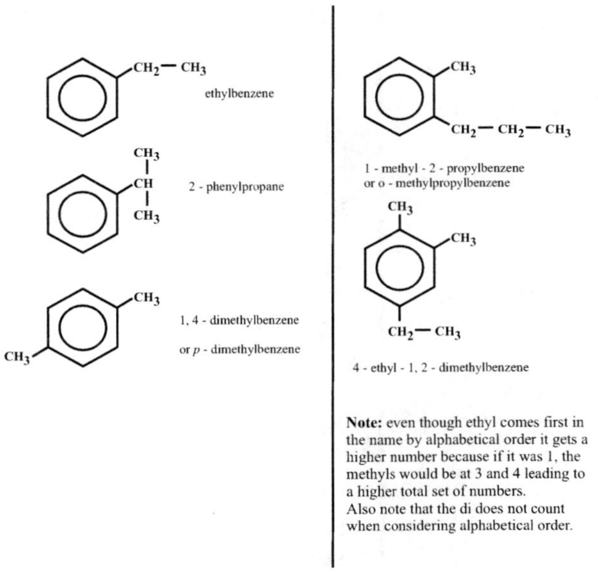

Isomerism

The phenomenon of existence of chemical compounds that have the same molecular formula but different molecular structures or different arrangements of atoms in space is called isomerism.

Structural Isomerism

Structural *isomers* are compounds with the same chemical formula but different bonds.

Other types of isomers are *optical isomers* and *geometrical isomers*, but we will only consider structural isomers here.

Consider the compound C_5H_{12}. It would appear initially to have many different structural isomers, but actually there are only three. You will see this if you try to draw others and carefully find the real long chain. The three isomers are:

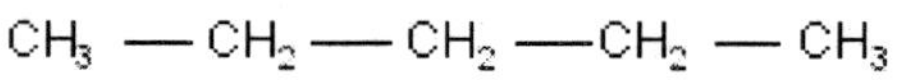

Pentane

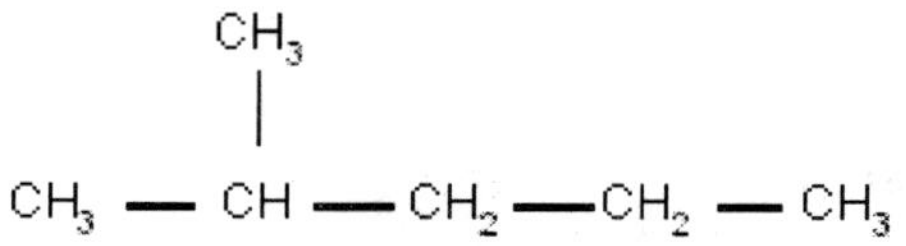

2-methylpentane

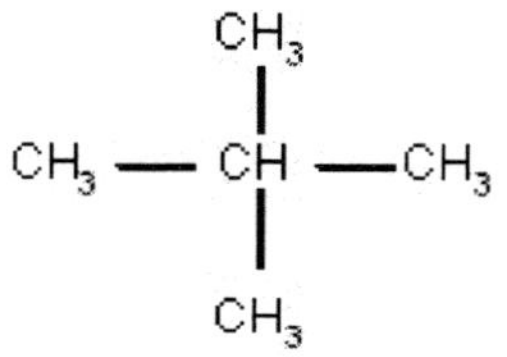

The numbers are not really necessary because there is only 1 place the methyls can go

dimethylpropane

Cis-Trans Isomerism

Cis-trans isomers are the compounds with same chemical formula but different position of groups with respect to double bond.

Cis Isomer

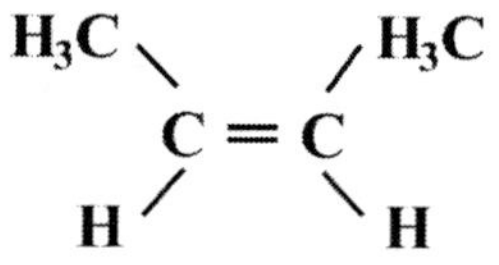

Trans Isomer

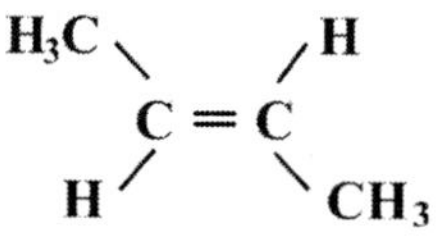

Related Questions: 1, 2, 3, 4, 7, 9, 10, 12, 14, 15, NR3

FUNCTIONAL GROUPS

7.3.1 Describe the term functional group and relate it to classes of compounds

7.3.2 Identify a compound as an alcohol, aldehyde, ketone, ether, organic acid, ester, amine, or amide when given a structural diagram

7.3.3 Name and draw structures for simple alcohols

7.3.4 Describe how an ester can be prepared through the reaction of an alcohol and an organic acid and how it can be detected (by its aroma)

Esterification

Esterification occurs between *alcohols* and *carboxylic acids*. As the alcohol and carboxylic acid react, H comes off from the alcohol and OH off from the acid to form water. The remaining fragments join together to make the ester. An acid catalyst and heat are required. Esters often have pleasant odours.

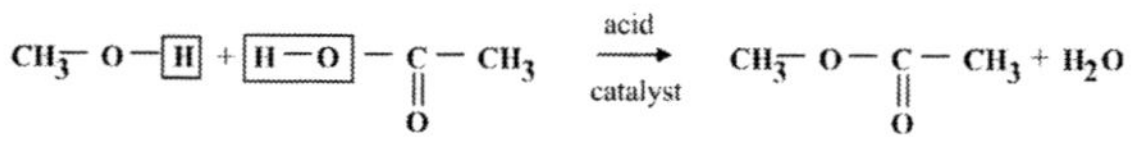

Related Questions: 5, 6, 11, NR1, NR2, NR4

Use the following information to answer the next question.

Paraffin is another name for alkanes. The name is derived from the Latin terms *parum* and *affino*, which together mean “chemically inactive”.

1. Alkanes might be considered chemically inactive because they

   A. are capable of accepting more hydrogen

   B. are unsaturated

   C. are polyunsaturated

   D. react extremely slowly under normal conditions because their C-H bonds are strong

Use the following information to answer the next two questions.

Computers are playing an expanding role in modern chemical research. Graduates from computer colleges, such as CDI College of Business and Technology, can find opportunities to work in this field if they have a background in chemistry. These graduates play an important role in creating software applications for controlling chemical devices and creating databases.

2. A CDI student has designed a program to enumerate the members of both alkenes and alkynes. Her program indicates that the third member of the homologous series of **alkenes** (general formula C_nH_{2n}) is

A. C_3H_6

B. C_4H_8

C. C_5H_{10}

D. C_6H_{12}

3. Her program would indicate that the third member of homologous series of **alkynes** (general formula C_nH_{2n-2}) is

A. C_3H_4

B. C_4H_6

C. C_5H_{10}

D. C_6H_{12}

Use the following information to answer the next three questions.

Gasoline must meet more stringent requirements as more and more government restrictions are placed on automobiles to increase fuel economy and reduce emissions. Catalytic converters, which oxidize unburned hydrocarbons and carbon monoxide and reduce nitrogen oxides, require compounds, like the following, to work more efficiently.

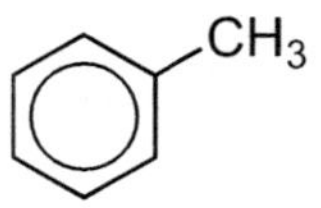

I

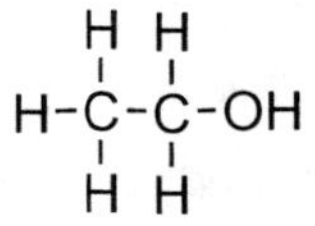

II

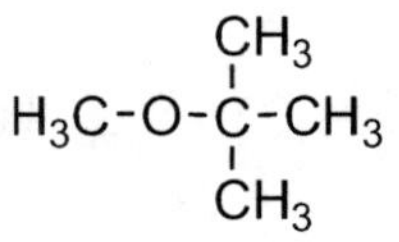

III

4. Compound I is

A. phenol

B. benzene

C. methylbenzene

D. cyclohexene

5. Compound II is

A. isoethane

B. ethanol

C. ethane

D. ethene

6. Compound III is

A. an alcohol

B. an ester

C. an ether

D. an aldehyde

Use the following information to answer the next question.

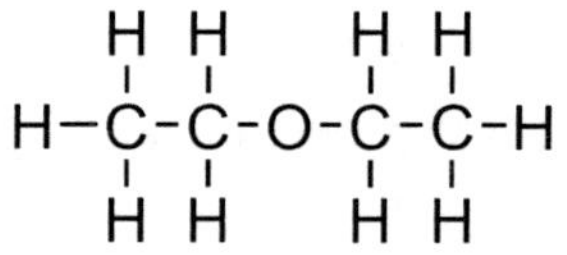

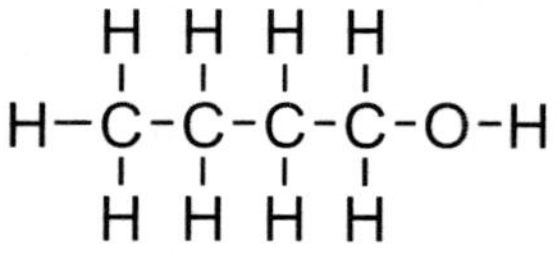

diethylether 1-butanol

7. The above compounds are

A. geometric isomers

B. molecular isomers

C. structural isomers

D. optical isomers

Use the following information to answer the next question.

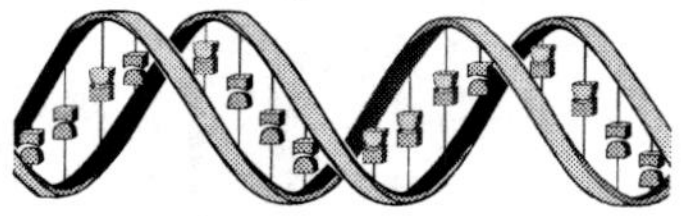

Recently, it was discovered that carbon-containing molecules can survive the frigid (50° K and lower) high vacuum conditions of outer space. In laboratory tests, DNA has been shown to survive these interstellar conditions. The unusual molecules C_3 and C_5 have been identified by astronomers who study microwave radiation from space.

8. If these chains were saturated with hydrogen, they would be known as, respectively

A. propane and pentane

B. propane and butane

C. butane and pentene

D. propane and pentene

Use the following information to answer the next question.

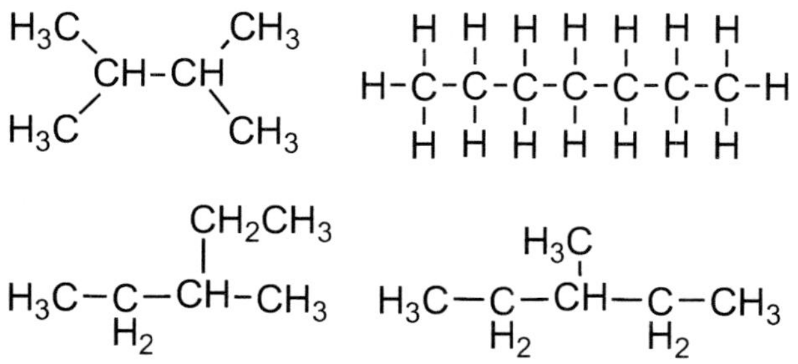

9. The number of different structural isomers represented above is

A. 1

B. 2

C. 3

D. 4

Use the following information to answer the next question.

Louis Pasteur discovered that two crystals of sodium ammonium tartrate, present in equal amounts in a mixture, were alike except for the fact that they were non-superimposable mirror images of each other.

10. Pasteur was describing molecules we now classify as

A. polymers

B. monomers

C. isomers

D. hydrocarbons

Use the following information to answer the next question.

Acetylsalicylic acid (ASA), found in aspirin, is a derivative of the active ingredient in willow bark tea, namely salicylic acid. Interestingly enough, Compound W™, a proprietary wart remover, is a concentrated aqueous salicylic acid solution. In aspirin, however, it was found necessary to modify salicylic acid to ASA to avoid the burning sensation salicylic acid causes when taken internally.

The structure of aspirin is

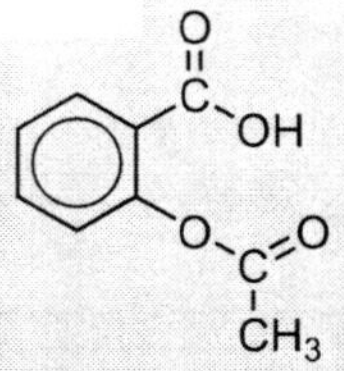

11. Two functional groups present in aspirin are

A. amide and amine

B. carboxylic acid and alcohol

C. ester and carboxylic acid

D. ketone and carboxylic acid

Use the following information to answer the next four questions.

1. propanol	**2.** propanal
3. propene	**4.** methyl propenoate
5. propanamide	**6.** chloropropane
7. propanoic acid	**8.** propyne
9.propanone	

Numerical Response

1. The number of **C**s, **H**s, **O**s, and **N**s, respectively, in the only nitrogen containing compound in the list above is ________,________, ________, and ________.

Numerical Response

2. The first four compounds (reading from 1-9) that contain a carbonyl group are ________, ________,________, and ________.

Numerical Response

3. In the list above, the alkyne, alkene, alcohol (alkanol) and aldehyde (alkanal), respectively, is ________, ________, ________, and ________ .

Numerical Response

4. The molar mass of the haloalkane in the list is ______________ .

(Record your answer to three digits.)

Use the following information to answer the next question.

Ethanol, used in the manufacture of poly(ethene), the plastic in grocery bags, is produced by the elimination of hydrogen from ethane.

12. An elimination reaction can be characterized by

A. two reactants exchanging parts to give two products

B. one reactant reacts so as to lose atoms, usually as a small molecule

C. two reactants combining to form a single product

D. a reorganization of bonds and atoms to give a different product with the same chemical formula

13. The complete combustion of methane would require
__*i*__ and would primarily yield __*ii*__ and
__*iii*__.
The blanks in the above statement are filled by

Row	*i*	*ii*	*iii*
A.	O_2	CO	H_2
B.	H_2	CO	H_2O
C.	O_2	CO	H_2O
D.	O_2	CO_2	H_2O

14. The reaction equation that correctly represents the combustion of butane is

A. $2C_4H_{10(g)} + O_{2(g)} \rightarrow 2C_4H_{8(g)} + 2H_2O_{(g)}$

B. $2C_4H_{10(g)} + 3O_{2(g)} \rightarrow C_2H_{6(g)} + 2CO_{2(g)} + 2H_2O_{(g)}$

C. $2C_4H_{10(g)} + 9O_{2(g)} \rightarrow C_2H_{4(g)} + 6CO_{2(g)} + 6H_2O_{(g)}$

D. $2C_4H_{10(g)} + 13O_{2(g)} \rightarrow 8CO_{2(g)} + 10H_2O_{(g)}$

Use the following information to answer the next question.

Naphthalene ($C_{10}H_{10(s)}$) is an aromatic compound that is commonly used in mothballs.

15. The complete combustion reaction of naphthalene is represented by

A. $C_{10}H_{10} + O_2 \rightarrow CO_2 + H_2O$

B. $C_{10}H_{10} + 12\frac{1}{2}O_2 \rightarrow 10CO + 5H_2O$

C. $C_{10}H_{10} + 12\ O_2 \rightarrow 10CO_2 + 5H_2O$

D. $2C_{10}H_{10} + 25O_2 \rightarrow 20CO_2 + 10H_2O$

Answers and Solutions – Introduction To Chemistry

1. A	**6. D**	**11. B**	**WR. 1-4 See Solutions**
2. B	**7. D**	**12. B**	
3. D	**8. B**	**13. C**	
4. B	**9. D**	**14. B**	
5. D	**10. A**	**15. A**	

1. A

The beaker has no label so although the solution may look like water it could just as easily be an acid or any other hazardous solution. The crack in the beaker means that it is weak and could break far more easily than a regular beaker causing a spill. The beaker is also sitting beside a lit Bunsen burner and may have recently been heated and is thus unsafe to touch.

2. B

Both the young driver and the science student are displaying by their actions that they have a conscious safety attitude. Either in a science laboratory or on the road, we are responsible not only for ourselves but also for the people around us. Though we may take measures to reduce or minimize accidents, we cannot definitively say that all accidents can be avoided. Therefore, the statement in B is not correct.

3. D

This is a situation requiring you waste no time and act immediately while informing the teacher and students of the danger. The other answers are not time efficient and/or do not involve dealing with the actual fire.

4. B

It is safest to immediately attempt to drop and attempt to smother the flames. Smothering is the quickest method of extinguishing flames available to you. If a person catches fire there is no time to move to the fire blanket unless you are already beside it. Damage from flames can occur at an alarming rate and flames can spread very rapidly.

5. D

The metre is the base unit for distance while the kilometre is a variation of metre.

6. D

Litre is the base unit of volume. Millilitre is a variation of litre but is not itself a base unit.

7. D

Conversion Factor:

$1 \text{ km} = 1000 \text{ m}$

$1 \text{ m} = 1000 \text{ mm}$

$\therefore\ 1 \text{ km} = 10^6 \text{ mm}$

$$2.5 \text{ km} \times \frac{1000 \text{ m}}{1 \text{ km}} \times \frac{1000 \text{ mm}}{1 \text{ m}}$$

$$= 2.5 \times 10^6 \text{ mm}$$

8. B

The conversion factor is:

$1 \text{ m} = 1000 \text{ mm}$

$$7.62 \text{ mm} \times \frac{1 \text{ m}}{1000 \text{ mm}}$$

$$= 7.62 \times 10^{-3} \text{ m} = 0.00762 \text{ mm}$$

This is equivalent to dividing 7.62 by 1000.

9. D

Conversion Factor:

$1 \text{ L} = 1000 \text{ mL}$

$$1.750 \times 10^5 \text{ L} \times \frac{1000 \text{ mL}}{1 \text{ L}}$$

$$= 1.750 \times 10^8 \text{ mL}$$

10. A

Grams are the metric unit of mass and when dealing with two masses with different prefixes it is easiest to do two separate calculations. This is true with any unit of measure. The first calculation would be from kilograms into grams and then the second is from grams into micrograms as follows

$$13.5\ \text{kg} \times \frac{(1000\ \text{g})}{1\ \text{kg}} \times \frac{(1 \times 10^6\ \text{g})}{1\ \text{g}}$$

$$= 13.5 \times 10^9\ \mu g$$

$$= 1.35 \times 10^{10}\ \mu g$$

11. B

In 0.078, the first two zeroes are place values and do not represent an actual value. Only the 7 and the 8 are significant figures in this case. All of the other values have 3 significant figures.

12. B

A compound is a group of atoms with an exact number and type of atoms arranged in a specific way. From the list given in the question:

i) Air is a mixture of different elements

ii) Methane is a compound with the chemical formula CH_4

iii) Water is a compound with the chemical formula H_2O

iv) Silver is an element represented by the symbol Ag

v) Carbon dioxide is a compound with the chemical formula CO_2

Therefore, II, III, and V are compounds.

13. C

Elements are pure substances which cannot be broken down further by chemical means. From the list provided in the question:

i) Zinc is an element represented by the symbol Zn

ii) Hydrogen is an element represented by the symbol H

iii) Brass is a mixture of Copper and Zinc

iv) Silver is an element represented by the symbol Ag

v) Soap solution is a mixture

Therefore, I, II, and IV are elements.

14. B

Heat is energy and as such the particles gain in kinetic energy and move faster. Temperature is the average kinetic of the particles in motion so an increase in kinetic energy means an increase in temperature.

15. A

As the translation energy decreases the bond lengths decrease and subsequently the molecules occupy less volume. The volume of the system is reduced.

Written Response

1. A pure gold nugget has a mass of 3.56 g and a volume of 0.184 cm^3. Determine the density of the gold nugget.

d = m/v

Therefore

$d = 3.56\ \text{g} / 0.184\ \text{cm}^3 = 19.3\ \text{g/cm}^3$

2. A 4.5g piece of iron is dropped into a graduated cylinder containing 10.2mL of water. Given that the density of iron is 7.9 g/cm^3, determine the new volume reading on the graduated cylinder.

Determine the volume of the piece of iron.

As $d = m/v$ then $v = m/d$

therefore $v = 44.5\ g/7.9 g/cm^3 = 0.57\ cm^3$

The piece of iron will displace the water in the graduated cylinder and raise its volume. Add the volume of water initially in the graduated cylinder to the volume of the iron. Remember that cm^3 is the equivalent of mL.

10.2 mL + 0.57 mL = 10.8 mL

3. Determine the number of significant figures for the following:

i) **120** has two significant figures, the last zero does not count as there is no decimal present and is a place value only

ii) **1.050** has four significant figures, all the zeroes are significant as they appear to the right of a non-zero value and there is a decimal present

iii) **0.345** has three significant figures, the zero does not count in this case as it precedes any nonzero digit

iv) **1010** has three significant figures, the zero between the 1s is significant while the last zero is not as there is no decimal present – it is only a place value

v) $\mathbf{6.02 \times 10^{23}}$ has three significant figures. All numbers when using scientific values are significant figures.

The $\times 10^{number}$ indicates place values.

4. Calculate the following showing the answer using correct significant figures.

i) 237050 × 3.41 = 808340.5 which is rounded to **808**000 with three significant figures, as 3.41 has only three significant figures and the answer to the operation can only have as many significant figures as the value with the fewest in the calculation.

ii) 435.00/0.03100 = 14032.25806 which is rounded to **1403**0 with four significant figures as 0.03100 has four and the answer to the operation can only have as many significant figures as the value with the fewest in the calculation.

iii)

$$\begin{array}{r} 23.1 \\ 2.55 \\ +9.367 \\ \hline \end{array} \qquad \begin{array}{r} 23.1 \\ 2.6 \\ +\ 9.4 \\ \hline 35.1 \end{array}$$

The values used cannot be more accurate than the least certain value which is the tenths position in 23.1. Therefore, using only values to the tenths for each of the other numbers, we get 35.1 as the correct answer.

Answers and Solutions – Atoms, Molecules, and Ions

1. A	**4. C**	**8. B**	**12. A**
2. C	**5. D**	**9. C**	**13. C**
3. D	**6. C**	**10. B**	**14. B**
	7. B	**11. B**	

1. A

A molecule is two or more atoms of any element chemically bonded together. They can be atoms of the same element or different elements so a compound is a molecule but not all molecules are in fact compounds.

2. C

Filtration is the easiest method of separating any solid from a liquid. Chromatography is primarily for separating dissolved substances from one another and distillation is primarily used to separate liquids from one another.

3. D

An ion is an atom or group of atoms that has gained or lost one or more electrons and subsequently is a charged substance.

4. C

This is an ionic compound and Calcium has a charge of 2+ while Fluorine has a charge of 1– so two Fluorine ions are required to bond with one Calcium ion to balance the charges. Remember in an ionic compound the positive and the negative charges are equal.

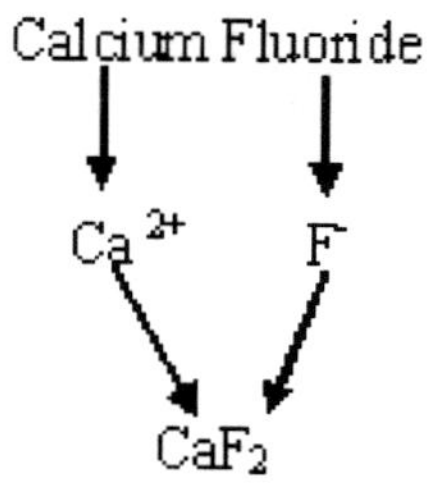

5. D

This is an ionic compound and Yttrium II means Y^{2+}, two positives charges. Permanganate has a charge of −1 and thus two permanganate ions are required to give the two negative charges needed to combine/balance the two positive charges on the Yttrium.

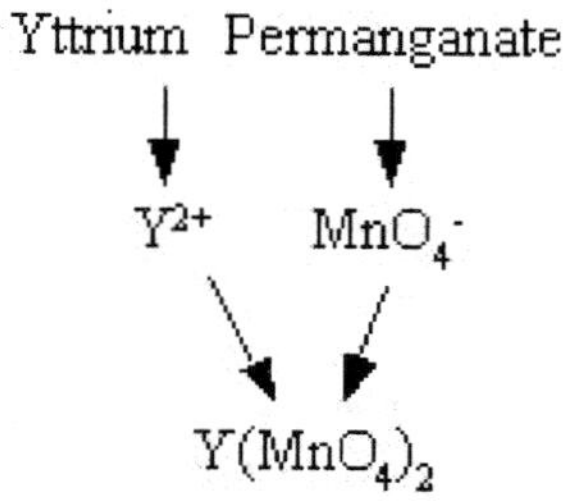

6. C

This is a covalent compound. Nitrogen has no prefix meaning there is one Nitrogen atom present while Oxide has the di prefix meaning there are two Oxygen atoms present.

7. B

This is an ionic compound with Manganese having a charge of + 6 and Phosphate has a charge of – 3, so two Phosphate ions are required to provide a – 6 charge to balance the Manganese's + 6 charge. Remember in an ionic compound the positive and the negative charges are equal.

8. B

This is a covalent compound. There are two phosphorus atoms present so the prefix *di* is used to indicate this and there are five oxygen atoms present so the prefix *penta* is used to indicate this.

9. C

This is an ionic compound. To name it you only have to give the name for the metal, Sodium, and the non-metal, Phosphate. The metal does not require a roman numeral to indicate its charge as Sodium always has the same charge. This compound has water molecules bonded to it and is thus a hydrate. A prefix is used to indicate the number of water molecules so ten water molecules is a decahydrate.

10. B

This compound consists of a metal and a non-metal and is thus an ionic compound. Ca is Calcium a group II metal with a consistent charge of +2 thus needing no roman numeral. F is fluorine and the ending is changed to "ide" in an ionic compound thus the proper name is Calcium fluoride.

11. B

This compound consists of a metal and non-metal and is thus an ionic compound. Vanadium is a metal that does not have a consistent charge and we must use a roman numeral to indicate its change in the name. O is Oxygen with a charge of -6 and there are three Oxygen atoms in the compound, so the total negative change in the compound is -6. The total change in an ionic compound must be zero so we can infer the total positive charge is 6. There are two Vanadium atoms in the compound so each must have positive charge of three to total positive 6 so the name is properly written Vanadium III oxide.

12. A

This is a covalent compound consisting of 2 nonmetals and uses prefixes to indicate the number of each atom present in the compound. There is no prefix in front of phosphorus indicating there is one phosphorus atom and the prefix *tri* in front of the chloride indicates there are three chlorine atoms. Therefore the compound is correctly written PCl_3.

13. C

Metals in ionic compounds have positive charges and Pb is lead a metal in this ionic compound. Carbonate is the non-metal with a charge of -2. There are two carbonate ions giving a total negative charge of -4. The sum of charges in an ionic compound is always zero so the positive charge total must be $+4$. There is one lead atom so its charge must be $+4$.

14. B

The acids containing hydrogen and non-metallic element are written with the prefix *"hydro"* and suffix *"ic"*. So, HBr is called Hydrobromic acid.

Written Response

1. a) Classify the following compounds as ionic or covalent.

i) ionic
ii) covalent
iii) ionic
iv) ionic
v) covalent
vi) covalent

b) Name the above compounds.

i) calcium fluoride
ii) carbon monoxide
iii) copper I chloride
iv) molybdenum II phosphate
v) silicon tetrafluoride
iv) diphosphorus pentaoxide

Answers and Solutions – Mole Concept

1. A	9. C	17. B	25. C
2. C	10. A	18. A	26. A
3. D	11. B	19. D	27. A
4. C	12. C	20. A	28. B
5. B	13. D	21. C	29. D
6. A	14. D	22. C	WR. 1-7 See Solutions
7. D	15. B	23. B	
8. A	16. A	24. C	

1. A

Specifically a mole is the number of carbon atoms, 6.02×10^{23}, in precisely 12.0 g of carbon – 12. There are other isotopes of carbon which have a differing number of protons and as such then a mole of any other isotope has a different mass. Moles of all substances are based on the carbon – 12 definition.

2. C

Converting from moles to mass, we get

$$2.00\,\text{mol Na}\times\frac{23.0\,\text{g Na}}{1\,\text{mol}}=46.0\,\text{g Na}$$

3. D

Converting from mass to moles, we get

$$32.0\,\text{g}\ CO_2\times\frac{1\,\text{mol}}{44.0\,\text{g}}=0.727\,\text{mol}\ CO_2$$

4. C

Unitary conversion from moles to molecules

$$1.50\,\text{mol NaCl}\times\frac{6.02\times10^{23}\,\text{molecules}}{1\,\text{mol}}$$

$$=9.03\times10^{23}\,\text{molecules NaCl}$$

5. B

Unitary conversion from atoms to moles

$$4.55\times10^{30}\,\text{atom Au}\times\frac{1\,\text{mol}}{6.02\times10^{23}\,\text{atom}}$$

$$=7.56\times10^{6}\,\text{mol Au}$$

6. A

To convert from mass to molecules we must first convert the mass to moles and then the moles can be converted to molecules.
Mass KCl $\rightarrow$ moles KCl $\rightarrow$ molecules KCl

$$10.0\,\text{g KCl}\times\frac{1\,\text{mol}}{74.6\,\text{g KCl}}\times\frac{6.02\times10^{23}}{1\,\text{mol}}$$

$$=8.07\times10^{22}\ \text{molecules of KCl}$$

7. D

$$1.00\times10^{-6}\ \text{mol}\ CaCl_2\times\frac{111.1\,\text{g}\ CaCl_2}{1\,\text{mol}\ CaCl_2}$$

$$1.11\times10^{-4}\,\text{g}\ CaCl_2$$

There are 3 significant figures in the starting substance and in any conversion the ending significant figures will be the same as the starting significant figures.

8. A

$$1.55\times10^{55}\ \text{molecules of}\ PCl_3$$

$$\times\frac{1\,\text{mol}\ PCl_3}{6.02\times10^{23}\ \text{molecules}}$$

$$=2.57\times10^{21}\ \text{mole of}\ PCl_3$$

9. C

$$584\text{ atoms} \times \frac{1\text{ mol}}{6.02\times10^{23}\text{ atoms}} \times \frac{197.0\text{g}}{1\text{ mol}}$$

$$= 1.91\times10^{-19}\text{g}$$

10. A

Simply stated Avogadro's hypothesis is equal volumes of different gases, at the same temperature and pressure, contain the same number of particles. This is a memory question.

11. B

At the same temperature and pressure equal moles of any gas will occupy the same volume. At STP, standard temperature and pressure, that volume is 22.4 L

12. C

This is a unitary conversion between moles of F_2 and volume of F_2

$$10.0\text{mol } F_2 \times \frac{22.4\text{L}}{1\text{mol}} = 224\text{L } F_2$$

13. D

This is a unitary conversion between mass and volume of a substance. Mass cannot directly be converted into volume and we must go through the unit mole. Any of the measures can be converted into moles and moles can be converted into any measure.

Volume in L $O_2 \rightarrow$ mol $O_2 \rightarrow$ mass O_2

$$50.0\text{L } O_2 \times \frac{1\text{mol}}{22.4\text{L}} \times \frac{32.0\text{g}}{1\text{mol}}$$

$$= 71.4\text{g } O_2$$

14. D

To determine the percent composition by mass of chlorine in Potassium pentachloride we would divide the total mass of the chlorine by the molar mass of the Potassium chloride and multiply by 100 to get a percent.

Mass of Cl = 5 × 35.5 g Cl = 177.5 g

Mass of PCl_5 = 31.0 g P + (5 × 35.5 g Cl)

= 208.5 g

% by mass Cl = (177.5g/208.5g) × 100

= 85% Cl

15. B

To determine the percent composition by mass of all the elements in the compound, KMnO4, we must divide the sum of the masses for each element by the molar mass of the compound and multiply by 100.

Mass K = 1 x 39.1 = 39.1g

Mass Mn = 1 x 54.9 = 54.9 g

Mass O = 4 x 16.0 = 64.0 g

Molar Mass $KMnO_4$=

39.1 g K + 54.9 g Mn + 64.0 g O = $KMnO_4$

O = 158

% by mass K = (39.1 g/158.0 g) × 100 = 24.7%

% by mass Mn = (54.9 g/158.0 g) × 100 = 34.7%

% by mass O = (64.0 g/158.0 g) × 100 = 40.5%

16. A

Step 1

We assume the mass of the compound analyzed to be 100.0 g so that the percent by mass of the elements is easily determined: 52.7g K and 47.3g Cl. Then we follow the procedure for finding empirical formula: grams → mol: find ratio and ratio is empirical formula.

Step 2	Step 3	Step 4
$52.7\text{g K} \times \frac{1\text{mol}}{39.1\text{g}} = 1.35\text{mol}$	K/1.34 = 1	1 K: 1 Cl – ratio is whole numbers therefore empirical formula is KCl
$47.3\text{g Cl} \times \frac{1\text{mol}}{35.5\text{g}} = 1.34\text{mol}$	Cl/1.34 = 1	

17. B

Step 1

We assume the mass of the compound analyzed to be 100.0 g so that the percent by mass of the elements is easily determined: 53.7 g Fe and 46.3 g S. Then we follow the procedure for finding empirical formula: grams → mol: find ratio and ratio is empirical formula.

Step 2	Step 3	Step 4
$53.7\text{ g Fe} \times \frac{1\text{ mol}}{55.8\text{ g}}$ $= 0.962\text{ mol}$	Fe/0.962 = 1	$\times 2 = 2$ - both ratio numbers are multiplied by 2 to make them whole numbers as the S ration value was 1.5
$46.3\text{ g S} \times \frac{1\text{ mol}}{32.1\text{ g}}$ $= 1.44\text{ mol}$	S/0.962 = 1.50	Therefore the ratio is 2 Fe: 3 S and the empirical formula is Fe_2S_3

18. A

The molecular formula can be determined as long as you know the empirical formula and the molecular (molar) mass of the compound.

(mass empirical formula)$_n$ = molecular mass

$(46.0\text{ g})_n = 92.0\text{ g} \rightarrow n = 92.0\text{ g}/46.0\text{ g} = 2$

this is multiplied in against the empirical formula so $(NO_2)_2 = N_2O_4$ is the molecular formula.

19. D

The molecular formula can be determined as long as you know the empirical formula and the molecular (molar) mass of the compound.

(mass empirical formula)$_n$ = molecular mass

$(14.0\text{g})_n = 70.0g \rightarrow$ n = 70.0g/14.0g = 5

this is multiplied in against the empirical formula

so $(CH_2)_5 = C_5H_{10}$ is the molecular formula.

20. A

In order to find the molecular formula we need the empirical formula and the molar (molecular) mass. The molar mass is given but we only have percent by mass of the elements in the compound. The first thing that must be done here is to determine the empirical formula. Once that is done the molecular formula can be determined.

Step1

Assume the mass of the substance is 100.0 g so that the percent by mass of each element is equal to its mass in the sample.

Step 2	Step 3	Step 4
$92.3\text{ g C} \times \frac{1\text{ mol}}{12.0\text{ g}}$ $= 7.69\text{ mol}$	C/7.69 = 1	1 C: 1 H – ratio is whole numbers therefore empirical formula is CH
$7.7\text{ g H} \times \frac{1\text{ mol}}{1.0\text{ g}}$ $= 7.7\text{ mol}$	H/7.69 = 1	

Now to determine the molecular formula

(mass empirical formula)$_n$ = molecular mass

$(13.0\text{ g})_n = 78.0\text{ g} \rightarrow n = 78.0\text{ g}/13.0\text{ g} = 6$

this is multiplied in against the empirical

so $(CH)_6 = C_6H_6$ is the molecular formula.

21. C

Molar mass of $Al_2(SO_3)_3 \cdot 16H_2O$ is 582.3g

$\% H_2O = (16 \times 18.0g)/582.3g \times 100 = 49.5\%$

22. C

Assume the mass of the sample is 100.0 g so the % is the mass.

$$13.0\text{g Mg} \times \frac{1\text{mol}}{24.3\text{g}} = 0.535\text{mol Mg}/0.535 = 1$$

$$87.0\text{g Br} \times \frac{1\text{mol}}{79.9\text{g}} = 1.09\text{mol Br}/0.535 = 2.04 = 2$$

1 Mg : 2 Br, therefore empirical formula is $MgBr_2$.

23. B

Assume the mass of the sample is 100.0 g so the % is the mass.

$$25.3\text{g Cu} \times \frac{1\text{mol}}{63.5\text{g}} = 0.398\text{mol Cu}/0.398 = 1$$

$$12.9\text{g S} \times \frac{1\text{mol}}{32.1\text{g}} = 0.402\text{mol S}/0.398 = 1.01 = 1$$

$$25.7\text{g O} \times \frac{1\text{mol}}{16.0\text{g}} = 1.60\text{mol O}/0.398 = 4.02 = 4$$

$$36.1\text{g } H_2O \times \frac{1\text{mol}}{18.0\text{g}} = 2.01\text{mol } H_2O/0.398 \quad 1$$

$$= 5.05 = 5$$

Cu : 1S : 4O : 5 H_2O

therefore is $CuSO_4 \cdot 5H_2O$.

24. C

Molarity is a measure of concentration and is equal to the numbers of moles in a given volume M = mol/L. Molar concentration is another way of stating molarity.

25. C

Molarity is determined by the formula

$$M = \frac{\text{moles}}{\text{L}}$$

So molarity $\text{NaCl} = \dfrac{0.15\text{mol NaCl}}{2.00\text{L}}$

$$= 0.075\text{M NaCl}$$

26. A

This question is asking for the molarity of the NaOH. To calculate for molarity the units moles and litres are required. To solve for this question then the first step is to convert the mass of the NaOH into moles. The second step is to calculate the molarity.

$$20.5\text{gNaOH} = \frac{1\text{mol}}{40.0\text{gNaOH}}$$

$$= 0.5125\text{mol NaOH}/0.950\text{ L} = 0.539\text{ M NaOH}$$

27. A

When volumes are mixed the molarity of a solution will change. It changes because the molarity is volume dependent as it is a measure of the number of moles in a given volume. To determine the new molarity we us the dilution formula, $M_iV_i = M_fV_f$ where M is molarity, V is volume, *i* is initial and *f* is final. This basically finds the moles of the substance and divides it by the new volume.

$M_i = 2.00\text{M}$ $V_i = 0.1500\text{L}$ $M_f = ?$ $V_f = 0.1500\text{L} + 0.01000\text{L}$ $= 0.2500\text{L}$	$(2.00\text{M})(0.1500\text{L}) =$ $M_f(0.2500\text{L})$ $M_f = \dfrac{(2.00\text{M})(0.1500\text{L})}{(0.2500\text{L})}$ = 1.20 M HCl

28. B

Using $C_1V_1 = C_2V_2$, we can calculate the initial volume of $HCl_{(aq)}$ required.

$$V_1 = \frac{C_2V_2}{C_1} = \frac{100\,\text{mL} \times \frac{0.0400\,\text{mol}}{\text{L}}}{0.200\,\text{mol/L}} = 20.0\,\text{mL}$$

20.0mL of 0.400 mol/L are required to prepare the desired solution.

Standard solutions are prepared in volumetric flasks of the appropriate volume, in this case, 100mL. The instructions for preparing a standard solution are outlined in the solution chapter of most high school text books. To ensure a high level of precision, it is important to use quality glassware such as pipettes and volumetric flasks.

29. D

In order to prepare a standard solution of a solid solute, the important first step is calculating the mass of solute required.

$$n\text{NaCO}_3 = \frac{0.100\,\text{L} \times 0.0500\,\text{mol}}{\text{L}} = 0.00500\,\text{mol}$$

$$n\text{Na}_2\text{CO}_3 = 0.00500\,\text{mol} \times \frac{105.99\,\text{g}}{\text{mol}} = 0.530\,\text{g}$$

0.530 g a $Na_2CO_{3(s)}$ are required to make 100 mL of a 0.0500 mol/L aqueous solution.

Whenever a standard solution is prepared, it is best to dissolve the solute (if it is solid and crystalline) in half the final solvent volume with the aid of a glass stirring rod.

Written Response

1.

First we need the volume of the room – $1\,\text{m}^3 = 1 \times 10^6\,\text{cm}^3$. We know that $1\,\text{cm}^3$ = 1 mL therefore 1 L = 1000 cm^3 so then $1\,\text{m}^3$ = 1000 L and the room is then 30,000L .

$$30{,}000\,\text{L N}_{2(g)} \times \frac{1\,\text{mol}}{22.4\,\text{L}} \times \frac{28.0\,\text{g}}{1\,\text{mol}}$$

$$= 3.75 \times 10^4\,\text{g N}_{2(g)}$$

2.

Molar mass of $Ag(NH_3)_2F$ is 160.9 g

% Ag = 107.9/16.9 g × 100 = 67.1%

% N = (2 × 14.0 g)/160.9 g × 100 = 17.4%

% H = (6 × 1.0 g)/160.9 g × 100 = 3.73%

% F = 19.0 g/160.9 g × 100 = 11.8%

3. The empirical formula and the molar mass are known so we can go straight to the determination of the molecular formula.

$$(\text{NO}_2)_n = 92.0\,\text{g} \rightarrow (46.0\,\text{g})_n = 92.0\,\text{g} \rightarrow$$
$$n = 92.0/46.0 = 2$$

Therefore $(NO_2)_2 = N_2O_4$ is the molecular formula.

4. First we must determine the empirical formula so will again assume a mass of 100.0 g, and the percent will become the mass of each element.

$$40.0\,\text{g C} \times \frac{1\,\text{mol}}{12.0\,\text{g}} = 3.33\,\text{mol C}/3.33 = 1$$

$$6.7\,\text{g H} \times \frac{1\,\text{mol}}{1.0\,\text{g}} = 6.7\,\text{mol H}/3.33 = 2.01 = 2$$

$$53.5\,\text{g O} \times \frac{1\,\text{mol}}{16.0\,\text{g}} = 3.34\,\text{mol O}/3.33 = 1$$

1 C : 2 H : 1O

Therefore the empirical formula is: CH_2O

Now we can calculate the empirical formula.

So

$$(\text{CH}_2\text{O})_n = 60.0\,\text{g} \rightarrow (30.0\,\text{g})_n = 60.0\,\text{g} \rightarrow$$

n = 60.0/30.0

n = 2

Therefore $(CH_2O)_2 = C_2H_4O_2$

5. Use the formula :

$$M = \frac{\text{grams}}{\text{molar mass}}$$

→ M(0.3400 L)

$$= \frac{7.45 \times 10^{-2}\text{ g}}{942\text{ g/mol}}$$

then solve for

$$M = \frac{7.45 \times 10^{-2}\text{ g}}{(0.3400\text{ L})(94.2\text{ g/mol})} = 2.33\text{ M } K_2O$$

6. Use the formula

$$M = \frac{\text{grams}}{\text{molar mass}} \rightarrow (0.500\text{ M})(0.2000\text{ L})$$

$$= \frac{\text{g NaCl}}{58.5\text{ g/mol}}$$

then solve for g NaCl = (0.500 M) (0.2000 L) (58.5 g/mol) = 5.85 g NaCl.

7. This question is a dilution so we use the formula

$M_iV_i = M_fV_f$.

$M_i = 0.250\text{ M}, V_i = 47.0\text{ L}, M_f = 0.125\text{ M}$ and V_f is unknown. We are asked to find what volume of water must be added to dilute the 0.250 M solution to a 0.125 M solution. Using the dilution formula we can calculate the final volume of the solution and if we take the difference between the final volume and the initial volume we will have the volume added.

Solve for $V_f = \frac{M_iV_i}{M_f} = \frac{(0.250\text{ L})(47.0\text{ L})}{(0.125\text{ M})}$

$= 94.0\text{ L} \rightarrow 94.0\text{ L} - 47.0\text{ L} = 47.0\text{ L}$

Answers and Solutions – Chemical Reactions

1. C	11. C	NR1. 249
2. C	12. C	21. C
3. C	13. D	22. A
4. B	14. D	23. A
5. A	15. D	24. B
6. C	16. D	25. C
7. B	17. A	26. B
8. D	18. C	27. C
9. A	19. D	WR. 1 See Solution
10. B	20. A	

1. C

In a chemical reaction essentially what happens is the reactant atoms are rearranged in a different order to form new substances. The new substances will have different chemical properties and reactivity than the reactants that formed them.

2. C

The reaction is in a closed system meaning nothing is entering or leaving the reaction vessel. It involves no gases being consumed or produced so the mass of the reaction vessel and its contents can be taken before and after the reaction accurately. We cannot measure the mass of a gas directly. A chemical reaction involves the reactant atoms rearranging to form the products so the mass of the reactants should, given the Law of Conservation of Mass, equal the mass of the products.

3. C

This reaction involves one reactant breaking down into two products. The only type of reaction involving one single reactant we have dealt with is the **decomposition** reaction.

4. B

C_3H_8 is a hydrocarbon and it is reacting with oxygen. A reaction of a hydrocarbon and oxygen that produces carbon monoxide and water is a combustion reaction. There may be other elements in the hydrocarbon than C and H and there maybe other products than carbon monoxide and water but if these factors are met is it a combustion reaction.

5. A

This reaction is a single replacement reaction. These reactions can be recognized by there being a lone element, Al, and a compound, Fe_2O_3, typically an ionic compound, as the reactants. The lone element will substitute for a like charged element in the compound: a metal will substitute for a metal and a non-metal will substitute for a non-metal. In the reaction in the question, the metal Aluminum is substituting for the Iron in the compound so in the products the Iron is now alone and the Aluminum is bound with the non-metal Oxygen.

6. C

Exothermic reactions release energy into the environment. The enthalpy of the reaction is negative as the products have less heat energy than the reactants did – there is an over all drop of potential energy in the system.

7. B

Firstly this is a synthesis and/or combination reaction. These reaction types can be recognized by there being two lone elements as the reactants, Mg and O_2 in this reaction, which combine to form a single compound as the product, MgO. The change in enthalpy for this reaction, $\Delta H - 285.8\,\text{kJ}$, is a negative value indicating the products have less enthalpy, potential energy, than the reactants. When energy is lost in the system it has been released into the environment and the reaction is called exothermic.

8. D

A balanced chemical reaction is necessary to reflect the Law of Conservation of Mass. Given that the reactants are rearranging to form the products there must be the same number of atoms of each element on the reactant side of the reaction as there is on the product side of the reaction. This of course is the reason that the mass of the products will equal the mass of the reactants as per the Law of conservation of Mass. We can only use coefficients to change the numbers of atoms of the elements as changing any of the subscripts will change what the actual substance is.

9. A

A balanced chemical reaction is necessary to reflect the Law of Conservation of Mass. Given that the reactants are rearranging to form the products there must be the same number of atoms of each element on the reactant side of the reaction as there is on the product side of the reaction. This of course is the reason that the mass of the products will equal the mass of the reactants as per the Law of conservation of Mass. We can only use coefficients to change the numbers of atoms of the elements as changing any of the subscripts will change what the actual substance is.

10. B

The complete neutralization of $H_2SO_{4(aq)}$ and $BaOH_{2(aq)}$ results in the release $Ba^{2+}{}_{(aq)}$ and $SO^{2-}{}_{(aq)}$ ions that combine to produce a $BaSO_{4(s)}$ precipitate. After examining a solubility table you will find that most sulphate compounds are high solubility except for those containing, $Ca^{2+}, Sr^{2+}, Ba^{2+}, Ra^{2+}, Pb^{2+}$, and Ag^{+}.

11. C

The reaction of $HCl_{(aq)}$ and $Mg(OH)_{2(s)}$ would be

$$HCl_{(aq)} + Mg(OH)_{2(s)} \rightarrow HOH_{(l)} + MgCl_{2(aq)}$$

Balance the atom or ion that is present in the greatest number, in this case, either OH^- or OH^- ions.

$$2\,HCl_{(aq)} + Mg(OH)_{2(s)} \rightarrow HOH_{(l)} + MgCl_{2(aq)}$$

Then balance the OH^+ ions.

$$2\,HCl_{(aq)} + Mg(OH)_{2(s)} \rightarrow 2\,HOH_{(l)} + MgCl_{2(aq)}$$

The answer is C.

Note: We can also solve this question by elimination since C is the only equation of the four presented that is balanced.

12. C

This question asks what the mole ratio of $HCl_{(aq)}$ to $Mg(OH)_{2(s)}$ is in the neutralization reaction

$$2\,HCl_{(aq)} + Mg(OH)_{2(s)} \rightarrow 2\,H_2O_{(l)} + MgCl_{(aq)}$$

2 and 1 are the coefficients of $HCl_{(aq)}$ and $Mg(OH)_{2(s)}$, respectively, in the balanced equation above.

Therefore, $\dfrac{n_{\text{HCl}}}{n_{\text{Mg(OH)}_2}} = \dfrac{2\,\text{mol}}{1\,\text{mol}} = \dfrac{2}{1}$ or 2:1

2 moles of are required to neutralize 1 mole of $Mg(OH)_{2(s)}$.

13. D

There are only two rules for balancing simple chemical equations by inspection

1) balance the species in greatest amount.

2) repeat rule (1) until all the atoms are balanced on each side of the equation arrow.

If normal balancing rules are followed we get

$2\,LiOH_{(s)} + CO_{2(g)} \rightarrow Li_2CO_{3(s)} + H_2O_{9(g)}$

The mole ratio is

$\frac{n_{LiOH}}{n_{Li_2CO}} = \frac{2\,mol}{1\,mol} = \frac{2}{1}$ or 2:1

14. D

An analysis that detects the *presence* of a chemical but not its *concentration* is a qualitative analysis.

15. D

Both $NaOH_{(aq)}$ and $HCl_{(aq)}$ are strong electrolytes that are completely dissociated in aqueous solution.

$HCl_{(aq)} \rightarrow H^+{}_{(aq)} + Cl^-{}_{(aq)}$

$NaOH_{(aq)} \rightarrow Na^+{}_{(aq)} + OH^-{}_{(aq)}$

The dissolved ions in the reaction are

$H^+{}_{(aq)}$ and $Cl^-{}_{(aq)}$, $Na^+{}_{(aq)}$ and $OH^-{}_{(aq)}$

16. D

There are only two rules for balancing simple chemical equations by inspection:

1) balance the species in greatest amount

2) repeat rule (1) until all the atoms are balanced on each side of the equation arrow.

When equation 1 is balanced we get

$6\,KAl(SO_4)_2 \rightarrow 3\,K_2SO_4 + 3\,Al_2O_3\ 9\,SO_3$

Therefore, the mole ratio of Al to Al_2O_3 is

$\frac{n_{KAl(SO_4)_2}}{n_{Al_2O_3}} = \frac{6\,mol}{3\,mol} = \frac{2}{1}$ or 2:1

17. A

Normally, water produced during combustion is hot and disperses as an invisible vapour. However, when it leaves a chimney in winter it cools producing a cloud of liquid water. Car exhaust is visible in winter for the same reason.

18. C

Photosynthesis is endothermic, since energy enters the reaction in the form of light.

19. D

A is incorrect since calcium, a metal, is (s).

B is incorrect since H^+, the positive ion of acids, is always aqueous (*aq*).

C is incorrect since the solubility chart shows $CaCO_3$ has low solubility (s).

D has the correct states of matter.

20. A

The balanced form of the equation is

$CaCO_3 + 2\,H^+ \rightarrow H_2O + CO_2Ca$

Therefore, the coefficients are 1, 2, 1, 1, and 1.

NR1. 249

To classify the following butane reaction:

$2\,C_4H_{10(g)} + 13\,O_{2(g)} \rightarrow 8\,CO_{2(g)} + 10\,H_2O_{(g)}$

recall the following definitions:

1. A *physical change* is one in which no new substances are formed.
2. A *chemical change* is one in which matter changes to produce new substances. CO_2 and H_2O are new substances.
3. An *endothermic reaction* is one that absorbs energy from its surroundings.

4. An *exothermic reaction* is one that releases energy from its surroundings. Burning releases heat energy.
5. A *formation reaction* is one in which simple elements combine to form larger, more complex compounds.
6. A *decomposition reaction* is one that produces products that are simpler than the reactants.
7. *A single replacement reaction* is one in which there is an exchange of one ion between the reactants to form products that are neither more nor less complex than the reactants.
8. A *double replacement reaction* is one in which there is a simultaneous exchange of two ions between the reactants to form products that are neither more nor less complex than the reactants.
9. A *combustion reaction* is a chemical reaction of a substance with oxygen that produces energy. This is combustion.

Therefore, the reaction of butane with oxygen, which produces new substances (carbon dioxide and water) and which releases heat to its surroundings, can be classified as a *chemical, exothermic, combustion* reaction, which are items 2, 4, and 9 respectively.

21. C

The coefficients used to balance the chemical reaction indicates the number of moles of each substance that are reacting with one another and being produced. In the reaction in the question, it is one mole of copper reacting with two moles of silver nitrate to produce two moles of silver and one mole of copper II nitrate.

22. A

First off the question asks for an amount produced so the only possible answers are a, b and c as d is a reactant. We see that $2\,AgNO_3$ reacts to produce 2 Ag which is a 1:1 ratio, so if 1.5×10^{-2} mol $AgNO_3$ reacted it could produce 1.5×10^{-2} mol Ag. No answers match this meaning it is an answer involving $Cu(NO_3)_2$. The reaction shows $2\,AgNO_3$ reacts to produce $1\,Cu(NO_3)_2$ so half as much copper II nitrate would be produced thus the answer is A.

23. A

The limiting reagent is the reactant that is consumed first and thus stops the reaction and limits the amount of the product that can be produced. We can use molar ratio numbers to see how many moles of $AgNO_3$ are required to react with the 1.8 mol Cu in the question.

$$\frac{Cu}{1.8\,mol} = \frac{2AgNO_3}{x}$$

x = the moles $AgNO_3$ required to react with 1.8 mol Cu

$x = 3.6$ mol $AgNO_3$ as we only have 2.9 mol $AgNO_3$ it is the limiting reagent.

24. B

We are calculating from mol of potassium nitrate to volume of oxygen.

Plan: mol KNO_3 $\rightarrow$ mol O_2 $\rightarrow$ volume O_2

$$0.500 \text{ mol } KNO_3 \times \frac{1\,O_2}{2\,KNO_3} \times \frac{22.4\,L\,O_2}{1\,mol\,O_2}$$

$= 5.600$ L O_2

25. C

We are calculating from mass of calcium hydroxide to mass of water.

Plan: mass $Ca(OH)_2$ $\rightarrow$ mol $Ca(OH)_2$ $\rightarrow$ mol H_2O_2 $\rightarrow$ mass H_2O

$$25.0\text{g Ca(OH)}_2 \times \frac{1\text{mol Ca(OH)}_2}{74.1\text{g Ca(OH)}_2} \times$$

$$\frac{2\text{H}_2\text{O}}{1\text{Ca(OH)}_2} \times \frac{18.0\text{g H}_2\text{O}}{1\text{mol H}_2\text{O}} = 12.1\text{g H}_2\text{O}$$

26. B

We are calculating from molarity of sodium chloride to mass of silver chloride.

Plan: molarity NaCl $\rightarrow$ mol NaCl $\rightarrow$ mol AgCl $\rightarrow$ mass AgCl

0.200 M NaCl $\times$ 0.0100L

$$\times \frac{1\text{AgCl}}{1\text{NaCl}} \times \frac{143.4\text{g AgCl}}{1\text{mol AgCl}} = 0.287\text{g AgCl}$$

27. C

$$0.0255\text{g H}_2\text{S} \times \frac{1\text{mol H}_2\text{S}}{34.1\text{g H}_2\text{S}} \times \frac{2\text{Ag}_2\text{S}}{2\text{H}_2\text{S}} \times$$

$$\frac{247.9\text{g Ag}_2\text{S}}{1\text{mol Ag}_2\text{S}} = 0.185\text{g Ag}_2\text{S}$$

Written Response

1. What is the limited reagent if 10.0 g of Al react with 15.0 g of Chlorine and what mass of $AlCl_3$ could theoretically by produced?

First determine the limiting reagent

$$10.0\text{g Al} \times \frac{1\text{mol Al}}{27.0\text{g Al}} \times \frac{3\text{Cl}_2}{2\text{Al}} \times \frac{71.0\text{g Cl}_2}{1\text{mol Cl}_2}$$

$$= 39.4\text{ g Cl}_2$$

39.4 g of Cl_2 is required to react with all the Al and only 15.0 g Cl_2 is present therefore the Chlorine will run out first and is the limiting reagent.

Second find theoretical yield of $AlCl_3$ from the Cl_2.

$$15.0\text{g Cl}_2 \times \frac{1\text{mol Cl}_2}{70.0\text{g Cl}_2} \times \frac{2\text{AlCl}_3}{3\text{Cl}_2} \times \frac{133.5\text{g AlCl}_3}{1\text{mol AlCl}_3}$$

$$= 191\text{ g AlCl}_3$$

Answers and Solutions – Atomic Theory

1. C	**11. C**	**21. B**	**30. B**
2. A	**12. A**	**22. A**	**31. A**
3. C	**13. A**	**23. C**	**32. C**
4. A	**14. A**	**24. D**	**33. A**
5. B	**15. A**	**25. D**	**34. B**
6. C	**16. A**	**26. A**	**35. D**
7. B	**17. A**	**27. D**	**36. B**
8. C	**18. B**	**28. C**	
9. C	**19. C**	**NR1. 153**	
10. A	**20. C**	**29. A**	

1. C

Thomson was the first to determine that atoms contain negatively charged particles.

2. A

According to Bohr's model, electrons were restricted to a defined orbit around the nucleus of an atom.

3. C

The number of protons in the nucleus of any element's atom is equivalent to the element's atomic number. The atomic number of Iron is 26 therefore it has 26 protons in the nucleus.

4. A

The number of electrons in orbit about an atom is equal to the number of protons in the nucleus as an atom is neutral. The atomic number of Chlorine is 17; therefore, it has 17 electrons in orbit about its nucleus.

5. B

The neutrons and the protons make up the mass of the atom and have essentially the same mass equal to one. Therefore the mass of the atom minus the number (thus mass) of the protons will equal the number (and mass) of the neutrons. Recall number of protons is equivalent to the atomic number.

Number neutrons = atomic mass – atomic number

Number neutrons = 54.9 – 25 = 29.9 = 30 neutrons

6. C

F^- is an ion with a –1 charge. This indicates there is one more electron present than proton, electrons having a negative charge and protons having a positive charge. The number of protons never changes, therefore, the atom has gained and electron and the total will be the number of protons (atomic number) plus one.

Number electrons = atomic number + 1

= 9 + 1

= 10 electrons

7. B

Although Y^{2+} is an ion that has no bearing on this question. The number of protons does not change in normal chemistry, that is the domain of nuclear physics. The number of protons will equal the atomic number of Yttrium which is **39**.

8. C

The mass of an atom is essentially made up by the protons and neutrons as the electrons mass is relatively insignificant. The number of protons does not change in an element so the mass differences between isotopes of the same element are due to differences in the number of neutrons present.

9. C

The atomic mass as it appears on the periodic table is a relative average of the isotopes of the element.

Atomic mass = (fraction of isotope)(mass of isotope) + (fraction of isotope)(mass of isotope) + …

Atomic mass = (0.189)(10) + (0.811)(11) = 10.81 amu

10. A

Al is a neutral atom therefore the number of electrons is equal to the number of protons. The number of protons is equivalent to the atomic number which is 13. The electrons are placed into the orbits and sub shells filling the lowest energy levels first: Order of electron filling:

$1s \rightarrow 2s \rightarrow 2p \rightarrow 3s \rightarrow 3p \rightarrow 4s \rightarrow 3d \rightarrow 4p \rightarrow 5s \rightarrow 4d \rightarrow 5p \rightarrow 6s \rightarrow 4f \ldots$ remembering that s holds 2 electrons, p holds 6 electrons, d holds 10 electrons and f holds 14 electrons. The electron filling in Al will be $1s^2 2s^2 2p^6 3s^2 3p^1$

11. C

O^{2-} is an ion with a –2 charge indicating it has two more electrons than protons. Oxygen has an atomic number of 8 therefore it has 8 protons. The oxygen ion then must have 10 electrons and the orbits and sub shells are filled accordingly as $1s^2 2s^2 2p^6$.

12. A

The number of protons in an atom is equal to the atomic number of the element. The number of protons does not vary in an element so the fact that there is a -3 charge associated with the As does not alter the number of protons in the nucleus. It is the number of protons which defines the element.

13. A

The number of protons in the nucleus of the ion is equal to the atomic number of Rhodium which is 45. This ion has a +2 charge indicating that is has 2 more protons than it has electrons so the number of electrons would be 45 – 2 = 43. The mass of the atom is mainly composed of the protons and the neutrons so the number of neutrons can be found by subtracting the atomic mass(# protons) form the atomic mass: 102.9 – 45 = 57.9 = 58 neutrons.

14. A

The atomic mass of chlorine is 35.453 which is much closer to 35 than it is to 37. This indicates that there is relatively more of the ^{35}Cl isotope than there is of the ^{37}Cl isotope. Only answer A suggests there is more ^{35}Cl than ^{37}Cl.

15. A

A neutron has no charge while a proton has a positive electrical charge so their charges are different. Neutrons and protons do have very similar masses with the neutron being very slightly heavier than the proton.

16. A

If they are to be the same element then they must have the same number of protons. Isotopes of an element differ in mass by having differing numbers of neutrons, never protons. Changing the number of protons changes the element.

17. A

Si is not an ion, therefore the number of electrons is equal to the number of protons. The number of protons is equivalent to the atomic number which is 14 for Silicon. The number of electrons is then 14 as they equal the number of protons in a neutral atom. The electrons are placed into the orbits and sub shells filling the lowest energy levels first: Order of electron filling:

1s $\rightarrow$ 2s $\rightarrow$ 2p $\rightarrow$ 3s $\rightarrow$ 3p $\rightarrow$ 4s $\rightarrow$ 3d $\rightarrow$ 4p $\rightarrow$ 5s $\rightarrow$ 4d $\rightarrow$ 5p $\rightarrow$ 6s $\rightarrow$ 4f… remembering that s holds 2 electrons, p holds 6 electrons, d holds 10 electrons and f holds 14 electrons.

18. B

The atomic number reflects the number of protons that are present in the atom. Oxygen has eight protons in its nucleus whereas hydrogen has only one proton in its nucleus. Therefore, B is correct.

19. C

Carbon-14 and carbon-12 are isotopes of carbon.

Isotopes are elements that have the same atomic number (therefore the same number of protons) but different atomic masses. The atomic mass depends on the number of protons, and neutrons, in the atom. Since isotopes are not ions, the number of electrons is also the same as the number of protons. Therefore, since the number of protons and electrons do not change, **the only difference between isotopes of an element is the number of neutrons** that are contained in the nucleus of the atom. Therefore, C is the correct answer.

20. C

Recall the relative mass of the three fundamental particles found in an atom. The mass of protons, neutrons, and electrons are shown in the table in the next column.

Particle	Relative	Mass in grams
Protons	1836	1.67×10^{-24}
Neutron	1836	1.67×10^{-24}
Electron	1836	9.11×10^{-28}

Protons and neutrons have approximately the same mass, and both have a larger mass than electrons. Therefore, C is correct.

21. B

The maximum electrons that can exist at each energy level, starting at the lowest energy level, are 2, 8, and 8. Lower energy levels are filled first. Therefore, potassium's 19 electrons will be arranged in this order 2, 8, 8, and 1.

22. A

The basic period trend for atomic radius is increasing as you go down a group and decreasing as you go across a period from left to right. Given this the elements in the right hand top corner of the periodic table should have the largest atomic radii. Helium is in that area and as such is the best answer to the question.

23. C

The basic period trend for atomic radius is increasing as you go down a group and decreasing as you go across a period from left to right. These elements all appear on the left of the periodic table and K, Ca and Sc are in the same period. We can exclude Y as it is in a lower period and should have a larger radius because of this. As the radius decreases from left to right across a period, the element furthest to the right in the period should have the smaller radius so the best answer is Sc.

24. D

The sulphur ion has a charge of – 2 indicating it has two more electrons than protons. Given that atoms do not gain or lose protons and neutral atoms have equal numbers of electrons to protons it must have gained two extra electrons.

25. D

Group 15 N, P, As, Sb, and Bi all have 5 valence electrons. Their electronic configurations all have an outer s and p of s^2p^3. Remember the outer s and p are the valence, reactive, electrons and stability comes from a full valence. It requires less energy to gain three electrons than it does to lose 5 electrons so the common charge would be –3, that from gaining three electrons.

26. A

The actinide series includes the elements with atomic numbers 89 through 103. Uranium, atomic number 92 falls within the actinides.

27. D

This question requires knowledge of periodic table properties to predict the relative reactivity of an element.

Lithium and sodium are both members of the **alkali metal group** (Group 1) on the periodic table. In a group, all elements have similar properties. If lithium and sodium react with water, it is reasonable to assume that cesium will as well. In Group 1, the reactivity of the elements ***increases*** from top to bottom.

Cesium (Cs) is near the bottom of Group 1, and therefore we can predict that it is the most reactive element in that group, and would react the most vigorously with water.

28. C

The only difference between the four compounds— $RhPtF_6, KPtF_6, XePtF_6$, and $SePtF_6$ is the first element in each.

Therefore, to answer the question, we need to know the relative reactivity of the four elements Rh, K, Xe, and Se.

On the periodic table, we can locate the group that each element belongs to.

Rh—Group 9

K—Group 1

Xe—Group 18

Se—Group 16

As Xe belongs to group 18 (noble gases), it would be the least reactive of the elements. Therefore, the correct answer is C.

NR1. 1 5 3

After internal differentiation, the elements in the unknown planet would have arranged themselves in order, with the heaviest closest to the core.

From the Periodic Table, the atomic weight of each of the seven elements is given below.

Region	Element	Atomic Weight (g)
7	gold	196.97
6	zinc	65.38
5	iron	55.85
4	sulfur	32.06
3	sodium	22.99
2	neon	20.18
1	helium	4.00

Therefore, helium, iron, and sodium are in regions 1, 5, and 3 respectively.

29. A

Basically chemical bonding is the interaction between the valence electrons of the atoms where the "share" an electron pair whether that be equally or unequally.

30. B

In an ionic bond there has been a substance that has lost an electron(s) obtaining a positive charge and a substance that has gained an electron(s) obtaining a negative charge. It is the positive and negative charge that holds these two substances together.

31. A

When there is an electronegativity difference between the substances of more than 1.7 there will be an electron transfer from the substance with the lower electronegativity to the substance with the higher electronegativity. This results with a substance having a positive charge and a substance with a negative charge forming an ionic bond.

32. C

Carbon and fluorine are both non-metals so this will not be an ionic bond. We do not have the electronegativities of the elements so it is not possible to determine the exact nature of the bond, polar covalent versus covalent therefore the best answer is a covalent bond.

33. A

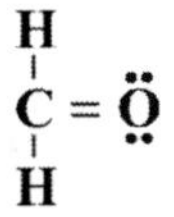

34. B

Sulphur has six valence electrons – its electronic configuration ends in $3s^2 3p^4$ which gives it 2 pairs of nonbonding electrons and 2 unpaired electrons available for bonding.

35. D

Chemical bonds form as atoms try to reach a more stable electronic configuration, typically that of the noble gases. Atoms are most stable when their valence is full and they will bond, share electrons, in order to come as close to this ideal as possible.

36. B

Carbon and Sulphur are both non-metals and are placed closely on the periodic table. Therefore they will have electronegativities that are fairly similar to one another and the difference between them is not going to be enough to significantly pull an electron from one atom to another. It is possible there will be some polarity in the bond but it is best described as covalent rather than ionic.

Written Response

1. Use the following compounds and your knowledge of the Periodic Table to determine the probable formula for a Hydride of Sulphur.

KH, CaH_2, Ga_2H_6, AsH_3, H_2Se, HBr

H_2S – we know that the elements in the same family – column – have similar characteristics and reactivity. Sulphur, S, is in the same column as Selenium, Se. The probable formula should have similar reactivity and predictability, and the same sort of bonding with Hydrogen.

Answers and Solutions – Solution Chemistry

1. C	5. A	9. A
2. C	6. D	10. A
3. C	7. B	
4. B	8. B	

1. C

A solution is a homogenous mixture where the solute and solvent appear as one substance and even share properties to a degree.

2. C

By definition the component of the solution which exists in the greater quantity is the solvent while the component in the lesser quantity is the solute.

3. C

Polar compounds go into solution best with polar solvents while nonpolar compounds go into solution best with nonpolar solvents.

4. B

An electrical current is conducted through a solution by electrolytes which are ions in the solution. It is ionic compounds that contain the positive and negative ions required to act as the electrolytes when the substance dissociates in the solvent to form the solution.

5. A

$CaCl_2$ will dissociate solution to form the positive and negative ions that make up the compound. It contains one calcium atom that has a charge of + 2 and two chloride ions that have a charge of – 1. The dissociation equation will must indicate the numbers of each ion formed and then charge on each ion.

6. D

The dissociation equation for the compound is:

$$K_2CO_{3(s)} \rightarrow 2K^+_{(aq)} + CO^{2-}_{3(aq)}$$

This shows us that two potassium ions are formed and one carbonate ion is formed. This means the concentration of the potassium ion, K^+, will be twice the starting molarity $(2 \times 0.500\,\text{M} = 1.00\,\text{M})$ and the carbonate ion, CO_3^{2-}, will the same as the starting molarity (0.500 M).

7. B

Answer a) this is a dilution problem coupled with a dissociation. We know it's a dilution as two volumes are added thus changing the molarities. We are looking for the $[\,Na^+\,]$ which is a component of NaCl so we will need to find its new concentration using the dilution formula; $M_iV_i = M_fV_f$

$M_i = 0.100\,\text{M}$

$V_i = 0.01000\,\text{L}$

$M_f = ?$

$V_f = 0.0100\,\text{L} + 0.1050\,\text{L}$

$= 0.250\,\text{L}$

(0.100 M (0.0100 L)

$= M_f$ (0.0250 L)

$$M_f = \frac{(0.100\,\text{M})(0.0100\,\text{L})}{(0.0250\,\text{L})}$$

= 0.0400 M NaCl

Next we write a dissociation equation for NaCl to and use the ratios from it to get the molarity of the Na^+ ion.

$$NaCl_{(s)} \rightarrow Na^+_{(aq)} + Cl^-_{(aq)}$$

There is one Na^+ produced so the molarity of the ion will be same as the compound it came from, 0.0400M.

8. B

The most soluble substances in nonpolar solvents are nonpolar compounds. The answer is B because Br_2 is a covalent compound thus nonpolar while A, C and D are ionic compounds thus form ions which are very polar.

9. A

For a solution to conduct an electrical current it requires charged particles. KCl will be able to conduct a current as it is an ionic compound and will dissociate in solution to for form ions.

$KCl_{(s)} \rightarrow K^+_{(aq)} + Cl^-_{(aq)}$. It is the charged ions that will carry the current through the solution. The other compounds listed are covalent and will not dissociate in solution to form ions and thus will not conduct a current.

10. A

The portion of a solution in greatest quantity is termed the solvent while the portion(s) in lesser quantity are termed the solute(s). In this case ethanol is 65% of the solution which is much greater than the 35% propanol forms thus ethanol is the solvent and propanol is the solute.

Written Response

1. Wanda combines two solutions, 125.0 mL of a 0.250 M solution with 175.0 mL of 0.450 M KI.
Determine the resulting concentration of the Potassium ion in the solution.

First calculate the molarities of the compounds after the dilution using the dilution formula
$M_iV_i = M_fV_f$

$$\text{Diluted } [K_2SO_4] = \frac{(0.250\,M)(0.1250\,L)}{(0.3000\,L)}$$
$$= 0.104 \text{ M } K_2SO_4$$

$$\text{Diluted } [KI] = \frac{(0.450\,M)(0.1750\,L)}{(0.3000\,L)}$$
$$= 0.263 \text{ M KI}$$

Secondly write the dissociation equations for the compounds and from them determine the concentration of the ions.

$K_2SO_{4(s)} \rightarrow 2K^+_{(aq)} + SO_4^-{}_{(aq)}$

0.104M so 0.208M 0.104M

$KI_{(s)} \rightarrow K^+_{(aq)} + I^-_{(aq)}$

0.263M so 0.263M 0.263M

$[K^+] = 0.208\,M + 0.263\,M = 0.471\,M\ K^+$

Answers and Solutions — Organic Chemistry

1. D	6. C	11. C	12. B
2. B	7. C	NR1. 3 7 1 1	13. D
3. B	8. A	NR2. 2 4 5 7	14. D
4. C	9. B	NR3. 8 3 1 2	15. D
5. B	10. C	NR4. 78.6	

1. D

Alkanes are saturated by (as many H per C as possible) and because C–H bonds are relatively strong they react extremely slowly under normal reaction conditions.

2. B

Member Alkenes	Structure	Formula
1st member ethene	$CH_2 = CH_2$	C_2H_4
2nd member propene	$CH_2 = CH - CH_3$	C_3H_6
3rd member 1-butene	$CH_2 = CH - CH_2 - CH_3$	C_4H_8

3. B

Member Alkynes	Structure	Formula
1st member ethyne	$H - C \equiv C - H$	C_2H_2
2nd member propyne	$H - C \equiv C - CH_3$	C_3H_4
3rd member 1-butyne	$H - C \equiv C - CH_2 - CH_3$	C_4H_6

4. C

Clearly, the compound I as shown is a substituted benzene compound—the substituent being a methyl group. The IUPAC name of this compound is therefore **methylbenzene.** (Its common name is toluene.)

5. B

The functional group in compound II is that of an alcohol. The second member of the alcohol or alkanol family is **ethanol**.

6. C

Compound III is an ether. Ether contains the functional group R–O–R, where R is a carbon containing portions of a molecule, such as CH_3.

7. C

The molecular formula for diethyl ether and 1-butanol is $C_4H_{10}O$. Two molecules that have the same molecular formula but a different structure are called **structural** or **skeletal isomers**.

8. A

Saturated hydrocarbons contain C and H bonded with single bonds only. This class of hydrocarbon is called the **alkanes**. The first ten hydrocarbons are listed below.

# of Carbons	Formula	Name
1	$CH_{4(g)}$	methane
2	$C_2H_{6(g)}$	ethane
3	$C_3H_{8(g)}$	propane
4	$C_4H_{10(g)}$	butane
5	$C_5H_{12(l)}$	pentane
6	$C_6H_{14(l)}$	hexane
7	$C_7H_{18(l)}$	heptane
8	$C_8H_{18(l)}$	octane
9	$C_9H_{20(l)}$	nonane
10	$C_{10}H_{22(l)}$	decane

9. B

Structural or skeletal isomers have the same chemical formula but different arrangements of atoms. Moreover, how you actually draw a hydrocarbon structure is open to interpretation. For example,

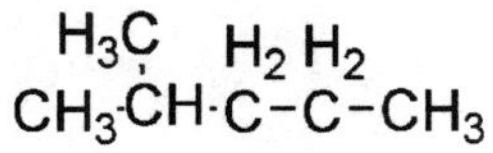

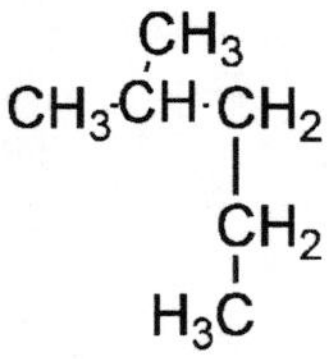

are the same molecules. Often, it is easier to label the carbons of the longest continuous chain of carbon atoms and name the molecules involved.

10. C

Molecules that have the same formula but different structures are called **isomers**. (Pasteur had in fact discovered what are now called optical isomers.)

11. C

The functional groups present in acetylsalicylic acid are a benzene ring, a carboxylic acid group, and an ester.

NR1. 3 7 1 1

In the list available, the nitrogen containing compound is propanamide: $CH_3CH_2CONH_2$ whose formula can be written as C_3H_7ON. Hence the answer is 3711.

NR2. 2 4 5 7

In the list available the carbonyl containing compounds are

2. propanal – an aldehyde/alkanal

4. methyl propanoate – an ester

5. propanamide – an amide

7. propanoic acid – a carboxylic acid

9. propanone – a ketone/alkanone

The structure of these compounds is shown below:

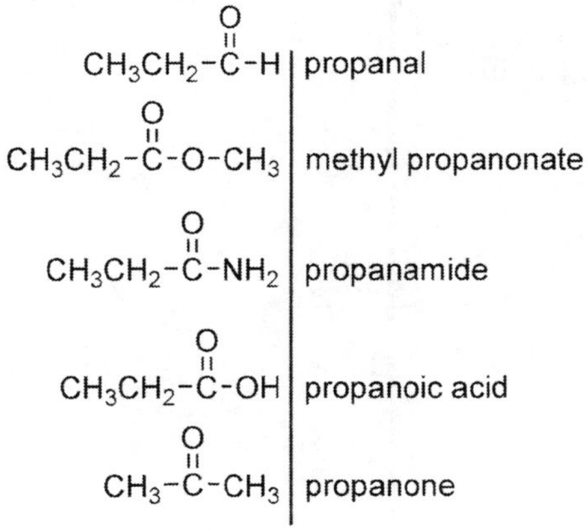

The four digit number corresponding to the first four carbonyl containing compounds is 2, 4, 5, and 7.

NR3. 8 3 1 2

The alkyne ends in the suffix -yne (propyne #8)

The alkene ends in the suffix -ene (propene #3)

The alcohol ends in the suffix -ol (propanol #1)

The aldehyde ends in the suffix -al (propanal #2)

The four digit answer is 8, 3, 1, and 2.

NR4. 78.6

A haloalkene is likely to contain the prefix fluoro-, chloro-, bromo- or iodo-. The haloalkene in the list is 1-chloropropene: $CH_3-CH_2-CH_2-Cl$, formula C_3H_7Cl.

The molar mass of this compound is

$(3 \times 12.01 + 7 \times 1.01 + 35.45)$ g/mol = 78.55 g/mol

The three significant digit answer is 78.6.

12. B

In an elimination reaction, a single molecule loses atoms or substituents on adjacent carbon atoms, essentially as a small molecule, and a carbon—carbon double bond is formed. For example,

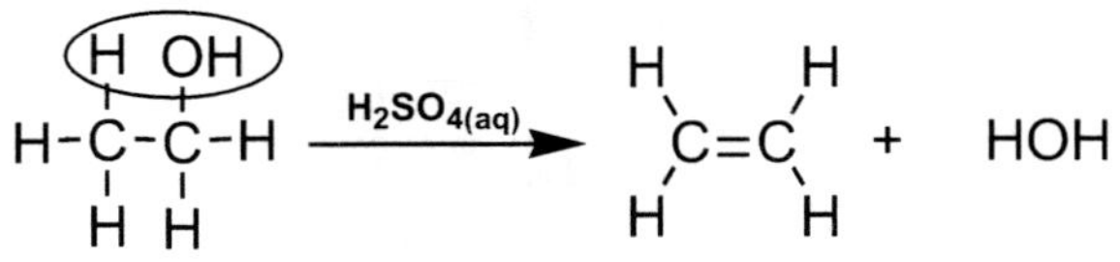

13. D

The complete combustion of methane would require $O_{2(g)}$ and primarily yield $CO_{2(g)}$ and $H_2O_{(g)}$.

14. D

When burning hydrocarbons (C and H only), it is important to ensure that an even number of moles of water vapour is produced so that a whole number of moles of $O_{2(g)}$ reacts. This often requires a doubling of the hydrocarbon.

15. D

When balancing the complete combustion of a hydrocarbon multiples of the reactant are often necessary to maintain a balance of oxygen on both sides of the reaction equation.

KEY STRATEGIES FOR SUCCESS ON EXAMS

KEY STRATEGIES FOR SUCCESS ON EXAMS

There are many different ways to assess your knowledge and understanding of course concepts. Depending on the subject, your knowledge and skills are most often assessed through a combination of methods which may include performances, demonstrations, projects, products, and oral and written tests. Written exams are one of the most common methods currently used in schools. Just as there are some study strategies that help you to improve your academic performance, there are also some test writing strategies that may help you to do better on unit test and year-end exams. To do your best on any test, you need to be well prepared. You must know the course content and be as familiar as possible with the manner in which it is usually tested. Applying test writing strategies may help you to become more successful on exams, improve your grades, and achieve your potential.

STUDY OPTIONS FOR EXAM PREPARATION

Studying and preparing for exams requires a strong sense of self-discipline. Sometimes having a study buddy or joining a study group

- helps you to stick to your study schedule
- ensures you have others with whom you can practice making and answering sample questions
- clarifies information and provides peer support

It may be helpful to use a combination of individual study, working with a study buddy, or joining a study group to prepare for your unit test or year-end exam. Be sure that the study buddy or group you choose to work with is positive, knowledgeable, motivated, and supportive. Working with a study buddy or a study group usually means you have to begin your exam preparation earlier than you would if you are studying independently.

Tutorial classes are often helpful in preparing for exams. You can ask a knowledgeable student to tutor you or you can hire a private tutor. Sometimes school jurisdictions or individual schools may offer tutorials and study sessions to assist students in preparing for exams. Tutorial services are also offered by companies that specialize in preparing students for exams. Information regarding tutorial services is usually available from school counsellors, local telephone directories, and on-line search engines.

EXAM QUESTION FORMATS

There is no substitute for knowing the course content. To do well in your course you need to combine your subject knowledge and understanding with effective test writing skills. Being familiar with question formats may help you in preparing for quizzes, unit tests or year-end exams. The most typical question formats include multiple choice, numerical response, written response, and essay. The following provides a brief description of each format and suggestions for how you might consider responding to each of the formats.

MULTIPLE CHOICE

A multiple choice question provides some information for you to consider and then requires you to select a response from four choices, often referred to as distracters. The distracters may complete a statement, be a logical extension or application of the information. In preparing for multiple choice questions you may wish to focus on:

- studying concepts, theories, groups of facts or ideas that are similar in meaning; **compare and contrast their similarities and differences**; ask yourself "How do the concepts differ?", "Why is the difference important?", "What does each fact or concept mean or include?" "What are the exceptions?"
- **identifying main ideas, key information**, formulas, concepts, and theories, where they apply and what the **exceptions** are
- memorizing important definitions, examples, and applications of key concepts
- learning to **recognize *distracters*** that may lead you to apply plausible but incorrect solutions, and ***three and one splits*** where one answer is obviously incorrect and the others are very similar in meaning or wording
- **using active reading techniques** such as underlining, highlighting, numbering, and circling important facts, dates, basic points
- making up your own multiple choice questions for practice

Numerical Response

A numerical response question provides information and requires you to use a calculation to arrive at the response. In preparing for numerical response questions you may wish to focus on:

- memorizing formulas and their applications
- completing chapter questions or making up your own for practice
- making a habit of **estimating the answer** prior to completing the calculation
- paying special **attention to accuracy** in computing and the use of significant digits where applicable

Written Response

A written response question requires you to respond to a question or directive such as "explain", "compare", contrast". In preparing for written response questions you may wish to focus on:

- ensuring your response **answers the question**
- recognizing **directing words** such as "list", "explain", "define"
- providing **concise answers** within the time limit you are devoting to the written response section of the exam
- identifying subject content that lends itself to short answer questions

Essay

An essay is a lengthier written response requiring you to identify your position on an issue and provide logical thinking or evidence that supports the basis of your argument. In preparing for an essay you may wish to focus on:

- examining **issues** that are relevant or related to the subject area or **application of the concept**
- comparing and contrasting two points of view, articles, or theories
- considering the merits of the opposite point of view
- identifying **key concepts**, principles or ideas
- providing **evidence**, examples, and **supporting information** for your viewpoint
- preparing two or three essays on probable topics
- **writing an outline** and essay within the defined period of time you will have for the exam
- understanding the "marker's expectations"

KEY TIPS FOR ANSWERING COMMON EXAM QUESTION FORMATS

Most exams use a variety of question formats to test your understanding. You must provide responses to questions ranging from lower level, information recall types to higher level, critical thinking types. The following information provides you with some suggestions on how to prepare for answering multiple choice, written response and essay questions.

MULTIPLE CHOICE

Multiple choice questions often require you to make fine distinctions between correct and nearly correct answers so it is imperative that you:

- begin by answering only the questions for which you are certain of the correct answer
- read the question stem and formulate your own response before you read the choices available
- read the directions carefully paying close attention to words such as "mark ***all*** correct", "choose the ***most*** correct" and "choose the ***one best*** answer"
- use active reading techniques such as underlining, circling, or highlighting critical words and phrases
- watch for superlatives such as "all", "every", "none", "always" which indicate that the correct response must be an undisputed fact
- watch for negatives such as "none", "never", "neither", "not" which indicate that the correct response must be an undisputed fact
- examine all of the alternatives in questions which include "all of the above" or "none of the above" as responses to ensure that "all" or "none" of the statements apply *totally*
- be aware of distracters that may lead you to apply plausible but incorrect solutions, and 'three and one splits' where one answer is obviously incorrect and the others are very similar in meaning or wording
- use information from other questions to help you
- eliminate the responses you know are wrong and then assess the remaining alternatives and choose the best one
- guess if you are not certain

WRITTEN RESPONSE

Written response questions usually require a very specific answer. In answering these questions you should:

- underline key words or phrases that indicate what is required in your answer such as "three reasons", "list", or "give an example"
- write down rough, point-form notes regarding the information you want to include in your answer
- be brief and only answer what is asked
- reread your response to ensure you have answered the question
- use the appropriate subject vocabulary and terminology in your response
- use point form to complete as many questions as possible if you are running out of time

ESSAY

Essay questions often give you the opportunity to demonstrate the breadth and depth of your learning regarding a given topic. In responding to these questions it may be helpful to:

- read the question carefully and underline key words and phrases
- make a brief outline to organize the flow of the information and ideas you want to include in your response
- ensure you have an introduction, body, and conclusion
- begin with a clear statement of your view, position, or interpretation of the question
- address only one main point or key idea in each paragraph and include relevant supporting information and examples
- assume the reader has no prior knowledge of your topic
- conclude with a strong summary statement
- use appropriate subject vocabulary and terminology when and where it is applicable
- review your essay for clarity of thought, logic, grammar, punctuation, and spelling
- write as legibly as you can
- double space your work in case you need to edit it when you proof read your essay
- complete the essay in point form if you run short of time

KEY TIPS FOR RESPONDING TO COMMON 'DIRECTING' WORDS

There are some commonly used words in exam questions that require you to respond in a predetermined or expected manner. The following provides you with a brief summary of how you may wish to plan your response to exam questions that contain these words.

- **EVALUATE** (to assess the worth of something)
  - Determine the use, goal, or ideal from which you can judge something's worth
  - Make a value judgment or judgments on something
  - Make a list of reasons for the judgment
  - Develop examples, evidence, contrasts, and details to support your judgments and clarify your reasoning

- **DISCUSS** (usually to give pros and cons regarding an assertion, quotation, or policy)
  - Make a list of bases for comparing and contrasting
  - Develop details and examples to support or clarify each pro and con
  - On the basis of your lists, conclude your response by stating the extent to which you agree or disagree with what is asserted

- **COMPARE AND CONTRAST** (to give similarities and differences of two or more objects, beliefs, or positions)
  - Make a list of bases for comparing and contrasting
  - For each basis, judge similarities and differences
  - Supply details, evidence, and examples that support and clarify your judgment
  - Assess the overall similarity or difference
  - Determine the significance of similarity or difference in connection with the purpose of the comparison

- **ANALYZE** (to break into parts)
  - Break the topic, process, procedure, or object of the essay into its major parts
  - Connect and write about the parts according to the direction of the question: describe, explain, criticize

- **CRITICIZE** (to judge strong and weak points of something)
  - Make a list of the strong points and weak points

- Develop details, examples, and contrasts to support judgments
- Make an overall judgment of quality

- **EXPLAIN** (to show causes of or reasons for something)
  - In Science, usually show the process that occurs in moving from one state or phase in a process to the next, thoroughly presenting details of each step
  - In Humanities and often in Social Sciences, make a list of factors that influence something, developing evidence for each factor's potential influence

- **DESCRIBE** (to give major features of something)
  - Pick out highlights or major aspects of something
  - Develop details and illustrations to give a clear picture

- **ARGUE** (to give reasons for one position and against another)
  - Make a list of reasons for the position
  - Make a list of reasons against the position
  - Refute objections to your reasons for and defend against objections to your reasons opposing the position
  - Fill out reasons, objections, and replies with details, examples, consequences, and logical connections

- **COMMENT** (to make statements about something)
  - Calls for a position, discussion, explanation, judgment, or evaluation regarding a subject, idea, or situation
  - Is strengthened by providing supporting evidence, information, and examples

- **DEMONSTRATE** (to show something)
  - Depending upon the nature of the subject matter, provide evidence, clarify the logical basis of something, appeal to principles or laws as in an explanation, supply a range of opinion and examples

- **SYNTHESIZE** (to invent a new or different version)
  - Construct your own meaning based upon your knowledge and experiences
  - Support your assertion with examples, references to literature and research studies

(Source: http://www.counc.ivic.ca/learn/program/hndouts/simple.html)

TEST ANXIETY

Do you get test anxiety? Most students feel some level of stress, worry, or anxiety before an exam. Feeling a little tension or anxiety before or during an exam is normal for most students. A little stress or tension may help you rise to the challenge but too much stress or anxiety interferes with your ability to do well on the exam. Test anxiety may cause you to experience some of the following in a mild or more severe form:

- "butterflies" in your stomach, sweating, shortness of breath, or a quickened pulse
- disturbed sleep or eating patterns
- increased nervousness, fear, or irritability
- sense of hopelessness or panic
- drawing a "blank" during the exam

If you experience extreme forms of test anxiety you need to consult your family physician. For milder forms of anxiety you may find some of the following strategies effective in helping you to remain calm and focused during your unit tests or year-end exams.

- Acknowledge that you are feeling some stress or test anxiety and that this is normal
- Focus upon your breathing, taking several deep breaths
- Concentrate upon a single object for a few moments
- Tense and relax the muscles in areas of your body where you feel tension
- Break your exam into smaller, manageable, achievable parts
- Use positive self-talk to calm and motivate yourself. Tell yourself, "I can do this if I read carefully/start with the easy questions/focus on what I know/stick with it/. . ." instead of saying, "I can't do this."
- Visualize your successful completion of your review or the exam
- Recall a time in the past when you felt calm, relaxed, and content. Replay this experience in your mind experiencing it as fully as possible.

KEY STRATEGIES FOR SUCCESS BEFORE AN EXAM – A CHECKLIST

Review, review, review. That's a huge part of your exam preparation. Here's a quick review checklist for you to see how many strategies for success you are using as you prepare to write your unit tests and year-end exams.

KEY Strategies for Success Before an Exam	*Yes*	*No*
Have you been attending classes?		
Have you determined your learning style?		
Have you organized a quiet study area for yourself?		
Have you developed a long-term study schedule?		
Have you developed a short-term study schedule?		
Are you working with a study buddy or study group?		
Is your study buddy/group positive, knowledgeable, motivated and supportive?		
Have you registered in tutorial classes?		
Have you developed your exam study notes?		
Have you reviewed previously administered exams?		
Have you practiced answering multiple choice, numerical response, written response, and essay questions?		
Have you analyzed the most common errors students make on each subject exam?		
Have you practiced strategies for controlling your exam anxiety?		
Have you maintained a healthy diet and sleep routine?		
Have you participated in regular physical activity?		

KEY STRATEGIES FOR SUCCESS DURING AN EXAM

Doing well on any exam requires that you prepare in advance by reviewing your subject material and then using your knowledge to respond effectively to the exam questions during the test session. Combining subject knowledge with effective test writing skills gives you the best opportunity for success. The following are some strategies you may find useful in writing your exam.

- Managing Test Anxiety
  - Be as prepared as possible to increase your self-confidence.
  - Arrive at the exam on time and bring whatever materials you need to complete the exam such as pens, pencils, erasers, and calculators if they are allowed.
  - Drink enough water before you begin the exam so you are hydrated.
  - Associate with positive, calm individuals until you enter the exam room.
  - Use positive self-talk to calm yourself.
  - Remind yourself that it is normal to feel anxious about the exam.
  - Visualize your successful completion of the exam.
  - Breathe deeply several times.
  - Rotate your head, shrug your shoulders, and change positions to relax.

- While the information from your crib notes is still fresh in your memory, write down the key words, concepts, definitions, theories or formulas on the back of the test paper before you look at the exam questions.
  - Review the entire exam.
  - Budget your time.
  - Begin with the easiest question or the question that you know you can answer correctly rather than following the numerical question order of the exam.
  - Be aware of linked questions and use the clues to help you with other questions or in other parts of the exam.

If you "blank" on the exam, try repeating the deep breathing and physical relaxation activities first. Then move to visualization and positive self-talk to get you going. You can also try to open the 'information flow' by writing down anything that you remember about the subject on the reverse side of your exam paper. This activity sometimes helps you to remind yourself that you <u>do</u> know something and you are capable of writing the exam.

GETTING STARTED

MANAGING YOUR TIME

- Plan on staying in the exam room for the full time that is available to you.
- Review the entire exam and calculate how much time you can spend on each section. Write your time schedule on the top of your paper and stick as closely as possible to the time you have allotted for each section of the exam.
- Be strategic and use your time where you will get the most marks. Avoid spending too much time on challenging questions that are not worth more marks than other questions that may be easier and are worth the same number of marks.
- If you are running short of time, switch to point form and write as much as you can for written response and essay questions so you have a chance of receiving partial marks.
- Leave time to review your paper asking yourself, "Did I do all of the questions I was supposed to do?", "Can I answer any questions now that I skipped over before?", "Are there any questions that I misinterpreted or misread?"

USING THE FIVE PASS METHOD

- **BROWSING STAGE** – Scan the entire exam noting the format, the specific instructions and marks allotted for each section, which questions you will complete and which ones you will omit if there is a choice.
- **THE FIRST ANSWERING PASS** – To gain confidence and momentum, answer only the questions you are confident you can answer correctly and quickly. These questions are most often found in the multiple choice or numerical response sections of the exam. Maintain a brisk pace; if a question is taking too long to answer, leave it for the Second or Third Pass.
- **THE SECOND ANSWERING PASS** – This Pass addresses questions which require more effort per mark. Answer as many of the remaining questions as possible while maintaining steady progress toward a solution. As soon as it becomes evident the question is too difficult or is tasking an inordinate amount of time, leave it for the Third Answering Pass.
- **THE THIRD ANSWERING PASS** – During the Third Answering Pass you should complete all partial solutions from the first two Passes. Marks are produced at a slower rate during this stage. At the end of this stage, all questions should have full or partial answers. Guess at any multiple choice questions that you have not yet answered.
- **THE FINAL REVIEW STAGE** – Use the remaining time to review the entire exam, making sure that no questions have been overlooked. Check answers and calculations as time permits.

Using the Three Pass Method

- **Overview** – Begin with an overview of the exam to see what it contains. Look for 'easy' questions and questions on topics that you know thoroughly.
- **Second Pass** – Answer all the questions that you can complete without too much trouble. These questions help to build your confidence and establish a positive start.
- **Last Pass** – Now go through and answer the questions that are left. This is when you begin to try solving the questions you find particularly challenging.

KEY EXAM TIPS FOR SELECTED SUBJECT AREAS

The following are a few additional suggestions you may wish to consider when writing exams in any of the selected subject areas.

English Language Arts

Exams in English Language Arts usually have two components, writing and reading. Sometimes students are allowed to bring approved reference books such as a dictionary, thesaurus and writing handbook into the exam. If you have not used these references on a regular basis, you may find them more of a hindrance than a help in an exam situation. In completing the written section of an English Language Arts exam:

- plan your essay
- focus on the issue presented
- establish a clear position using a thesis statement to direct and unify your writing
- organize your writing in a manner that logically presents your views
- support your viewpoint with specific examples
- edit and proof read your writing

In completing the reading section of an English Language Arts exam:

- read the entire selection before responding
- use titles, dates, footnotes, pictures, introductions, and notes on the author to assist you in developing an understanding of the piece presented
- when using line references, read a few lines before and after the identified section

MATHEMATICS

In some instances, the use of calculators is permitted (or required) to complete complex calculations, modeling, simulations, or to demonstrate your use of technology. It is imperative that you are familiar with the approved calculator and the modes you may be using during your exam. In writing exams in mathematics:

- use appropriate mathematical notation and symbols
- clearly show or explain all the steps involved in solving the problem
- check to be sure you have included the correct units of measurement and have rounded to the appropriate significant digit
- use appropriate labelling and equal increments on graphs

SCIENCES

In the Sciences written response and open-ended questions usually require a clear, organized, and detailed explanation of the science involved in the question. You may find it helpful to use the acronym **STEEPLES** to organize your response to these types of questions. STEEPLES stands for **S**cience, **T**echnological, **E**cological, **E**thical, **P**olitical, **L**egal, **E**conomical, and **S**ocial aspects of the issue presented. In writing exams in the sciences:

- use scientific vocabulary to clearly explain your understanding of the processes or issues
- state your position in an objective manner
- demonstrate your understanding of both sides of the issue
- clearly label graphs, diagrams, tables, and charts using accepted conventions
- provide all formulas and equations

SOCIAL STUDIES, HISTORY, GEOGRAPHY

Exams in these courses of study often require you to take a position on an issue and defend your point of view. Your response should demonstrate your understanding of both the positive and negative aspects of the issue and be supported by well-considered arguments and evidence. In writing exams in Social Studies, History or Geography, the following acronyms may be helpful to you in organizing your approach.

- **SEE** – stands for **S**tatement, **E**xplanation, **E**xample. This acronym reminds you to couple your statement regarding your position with an explanation and then an example.

- **PERMS** – stands for **P**olitical, **E**conomic, **R**eligious or moral, **M**ilitary, and **S**ocietal values. Your position statement may be derived from or based upon any of these points of view. Your argument is more credible if you can show that recognized authorities such as leaders, theorists, writers or scientists back your position.

SUMMARY

Writing exams involves a certain amount of stress and anxiety. If you want to do your best on the exam, *there is no substitute for being well prepared.* Being well prepared helps you to feel more confident about your ability to succeed and less anxious about writing tests. In preparing for unit or year-end exams remember to:

- use as many senses as possible in preparing for exams
- start as early as possible set realistic goals and targets
- take advantage of study buddies, study groups, and tutorials
- review previously used exams
- study with positive, knowledgeable, motivated, and supportive individuals
- practice the material in the format in which you are to be tested
- try to simulate the test situation as much as possible
- keep a positive attitude
- end your study time with a quick review and then do something different before you try to go to sleep on the night before the exam
- drink a sufficient amount of water prior to an exam
- stay in the exam room for the full amount of time available
- try to relax by focusing on your breathing

If you combine your best study habits with some of the strategies presented here, you may increase your chances of writing a strong exam and maximizing your potential to do well.

NOTES

Practice Exam

A guide to preparing for an exam

The questions presented here are distinct from those in the Unit Review section. **THE KEY** contains detailed answers that illustrate the problem-solving process for every question in this section.

Students are encouraged to write this practice exam under conditions similar to those they will encounter when writing their final exam. This will make students:

* *aware of the mental and physical stamina required to sit through an entire exam*
* *familiar with the exam format and how the course content is tested*
* *aware of any units or concepts that are troublesome or require additional study*
* *more successful in managing their review effectively*

To simulate the exam conditions students should:

* *use an alarm clock or other timer to monitor the time allowed for the exam*
* *select a quiet writing spot away from all distractions*
* *assemble the appropriate materials that are allowed for writing the exam such as pens, HB pencils, calculator, dictionary*
* *use "test wiseness" skills*
* *complete as much of the exam as possible within the allowable time*

In writing the practice exam students should:

* *read instructions, directions and questions carefully*
* *organize writing time according to the exam emphasis on each section*
* *highlight key words*
* *think about what is being asked*
* *plan their writing; once complete, proof for errors in content, spelling, grammar*
* *watch for bolded words such as most, least, best*
* *in Multiple Choice questions, cross out any choices students know are incorrect*
* *if possible, review all responses upon completion of the exam*

Practice Examination

1. Which of the following is not an SI unit?

   A. s
   B. mL
   C. g
   D. m

2. How many significant digits are present in 56070?

   A. 4
   B. 5
   C. 3
   D. 2

3. Considering significant figures, the correct answer for $\left(\frac{6.02\times10^{23}}{0.02457}\right)$ is

   A. 1.48×10^{22}
   B. 2.450×10^{25}
   C. 2.45×10^{24}
   D. 2.45×10^{25}

4. If a chemical reaction produces 0.0150g of CO_2 in 2.00 min, the rate would best be described in which unit?

   A. g/s
   B. g • min
   C. g/s^{-1}
   D. g^{-1}/s

5. What is the measure indicated on the scale below?

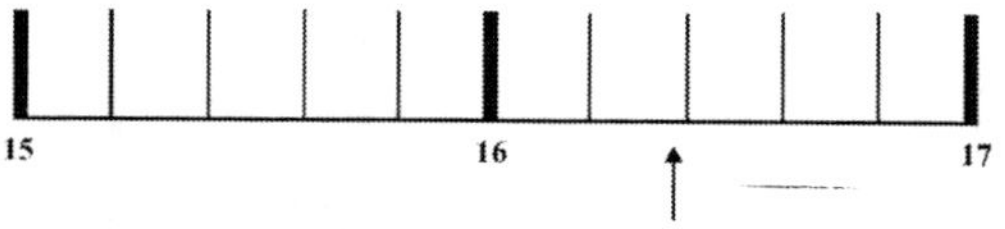

   A. 16.3
   B. 16.29
   C. 16.35
   D. 15.16

6. Matter can best be defined as anything that has __________ and occupies __________.

   A. mass, area
   B. volume, mass
   C. atoms, volume
   D. mass, volume

7. Matter can be identified by its __________.

   A. properties
   B. shape
   C. molecular structure
   D. coreolis effect

8. New substances with new properties produced describes

   A. a chemical change
   B. a physical change
   C. vaporization
   D. sublimation

9. Which of the following cannot chemically be separated into simpler substances?

   A. element
   B. compound
   C. solution
   D. polyatomic ion

10. The correct name for $KClO_4$ is

    A. Potassium Chlorate
    B. Potassium I Perchlorate
    C. Potassium Chlorine tetraoxide
    D. Potassium Perchlorate

11. The correct name for $Mg_2(PO_4)_2$ is

    A. Magnesium Phosphate
    B. Manganese Phosphate
    C. Magnesium II Phosphate
    D. Manganese II Phosphate

12. The correct name for SCl_2 is

A. Sulphur Chloride
B. diSulphur Chloride
C. Sulphur dichloride
D. Sulphur II Chloride

13. The correct name for PbO_2 is

A. Lead Oxide
B. Lead II Oxide
C. Lead dioxide
D. Lead IV Oxide

14. The correct chemical formula for Ammonium Oxalate is

A. $NH_4C_2O_4$
B. $(NH_4)_2C_2O_4$
C. $(NH_4)C_2O_4$
D. $NH_4(C_2O_4)_2$

15. The correct chemical formula for diphosphorus pentachloride is

A. P_2O_5
B. P_5Cl_2
C. P_2C_5
D. P_2Cl_5

16. The unit used to count the numbers of atoms, molecules or ions present is

A. the mole
B. the atomic number
C. the isotope
D. the joule

17. The molar mass of Yttrium is

A. 88.9 g
B. 88.9 AMU
C. 39 g
D. 39 AMU

18. The molar mass of $Mn_2(CO_3)_3$ is

A. 289.8 g
B. 289.8 AMU
C. 239.9 g
D. 239.9 AMU

19. How many moles are in 32.0 g CH_2O?

A. 960 mol
B. 0.938 mol
C. 1.07 mol
D. 0.107 mol

20. How many molecules are present in 0.150 moles of RbCl?

A. 9×10^{22}
B. 2.49×10^{-23}
C. 9.03×10^{22}
D. 9.03×10^{22}

21. How many molecules are in 1.63×10^{-3} g of KCl?

A. 7.32×10^{-22} molecules
B. 7.32×10^{22} molecules
C. 2.02×10^{-25} molecules
D. 1.32×10^{19} molecules

22. What volume would 75.0 mol $NO_{(g)}$ occupy at STP?

A. 1680 L
B. 168.0 L
C. 3.35 L
D. 56.0 L

23. What is the mass of 150.0 mL of $Cl_{2(g)}$ at STP?

A. 26.67 g
B. 238.5 g
C. 475.4 g
D. 0.4754 g

24. Phentylfloroform is 57.54% C, 3.45% H and 39.1% F. What is the empirical formula of the compound?

A. $C_7H_5F_3$

B. $C_3H_2F_1$

C. $C_5H_7F_3$

D. $C_7H_3F_3$

25. Molarity is a measure of

A. molar ability

B. molar volume

C. moles per mass

D. molar concentration

26. The molarity of a solution prepared by dissolving 0.350 mol KI in 2.75 L of water is

A. 1.27 M KI

B. 0.127 M KI

C. 0.963 M KI

D. 9.63 M KI

27. The mass of RbCl required to prepare 2.000L of a 0.4500 M RbCl solution is

A. 134.4 g

B. 7.34×10^{-3} g

C. 108.9 g

D. 18.9 g

28. If 150.0 mL water is added to 250.0 mL of a 1.00 M HNO_3 solution the new molarity of HNO_3 is

A. 0.625M HNO_3

B. 26.67M HNO_3

C. 0.400M HNO_3

D. 0.120M HNO_3

29. How do the masses of reactants and products relate if a reaction occurs in a closed system?

A. they are equal

B. they are proportionate

C. the mass of products decreases

D. the masses do not change

30. The following reaction can be identified as
$C_2H_5OH + O_2 \rightarrow CO_2 + H_2O$

A. combustion

B. single replacement

C. synthesis/combination

D. double replacement

31. The following reaction can be identified as
$AgNO_3 + NaCl \rightarrow AgCl + NaNO_3$

A. combustion

B. single replacement

C. acid/base neutralization

D. double replacement

32. The following reaction can be identified as
$KClO_3 \rightarrow KCl + O_2$

A. acid/base

B. synthesis

C. composition

D. decomposition

33. The coefficients for the following reaction to be properly balanced would be
$Zn + HCl \rightarrow ZnCl_2 + H_2$

A. 1,2,1,1

B. 2,4,2,2

C. 2,4,2,1

D. 1,2,2,1

34. The following reaction can be identified as
$H_2 + Cl_2 \rightarrow 2HCl + 185\ kJ$

A. synthesis and exothermic
B. synthesis and endothermic
C. decomposition and exothermic
D. single replacement and endothermic

35. Consider the following reaction:
$4NH_{3(g)} + 5O_{2(g)} \rightarrow 4NO_{(g)} + 6H_2O_{(l)}$
How many moles of O_2 are required to produce 6.0 moles of NO?

A. 4.8 moles
B. 7.5 moles
C. 6.0 moles
D. 5.0 moles

36. Consider the following reaction:
$Cu + 2AgNO_3 \rightarrow Cu(NO_3)_2 + 2Ag$
There is 16.0 g Cu and 42.0g $AgNO_3$ present in a reaction vessel. Which reactant is the limiting reagent?

A. Ag
B. Cu
C. $AgNO_3$
D. $Cu(NO_3)_2$

37. How many neutrons are present in the nucleus of a Neodymium atom?

A. 84
B. 60
C. 84.2
D. 90

38. The number protons in the nucleus of an Iridium atom are

A. 115
B. 192
C. 77
D. 78

39. How many electrons are there in orbit about the P^{3-} ion?

A. 18
B. 15
C. 31
D. 16

40. What is the electronic configuration of Titanium?

A. $1s^2 2s^2 2p^6 3s^2 3p^6$
B. $1s^2 2s^2 2p^6 3s^2 3p^6 4s^2 3d^1$
C. $1s^2 2s^2 2p^6 3s^2 3p^6 4s^2$
D. $1s^2 2s^2 2p^6 3s^2 3p^6 4s^2 3d^2$

41. What is the electronic configuration of Mn^{4+}?

A. $1s^2 2s^2 2p^6 3s^2 3p^6 4s^2 3d^1$
B. $1s^2 2s^2 2p^6 3s^2 3p^6 4s^2 3d^9$
C. $1s^2 2s^2 2p^6 3s^2 3p^6 4s^2 3d^5$
D. $1s^2 2s^2 2p^6 3s^2 3p^6 4s^2 4p^1$

42. Column 14 elements have an electronic configuration that ends in

A. s^2p^2
B. s^2p^3
C. s^2p^1
D. s^2d^2

43. Which of the following elements is a member of the Alkaline Earth metals?

A. Sr
B. Rb
C. Y
D. Xe

44. Which of the following is a property of a Halogen?

- **A.** conducts electricity
- **B.** very soft and malleable
- **C.** most are hard and dense
- **D.** diatomic in gaseous phase

45. Which element will tend to gain 3 electrons to have a noble gas configuration?

- **A.** C
- **B.** P
- **C.** S
- **D.** Cl

46. What type of bonding involves a partial electron transfer?

- **A.** ionic
- **B.** covalent
- **C.** polar covalent
- **D.** London's

47. What type of bond is present in PCl_3?

- **A.** covalent
- **B.** ionic
- **C.** double
- **D.** hydrogen

Use the following information to answer the next question.

Chlorine (Cl_2) is used in great quantity as a bleach for the pulp and paper industry and as a disinfectant for municipal water supplies. Iodine is another chemical commonly used for water disinfection on a smaller scale. The boiling point of chlorine is –34.6° C while the boiling point of iodine is 184° C.

48. The electrons involved in the bonding within chlorine molecules are

- **A.** completely transferred from one atom to another
- **B.** equally shared
- **C.** unequally shared
- **D.** the inner shell electrons only

Use the following diagram to answer the next question.

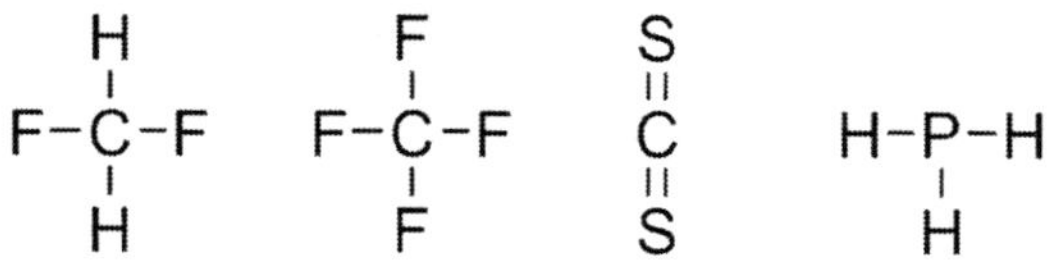

I II III IV

49. The polar molecule is

- **A.** I
- **B.** II
- **C.** III
- **D.** IV

Use the following information to answer the next question.

Acids have a characteristic sour taste. Foods such as lemons, oranges, and tomatoes contain citric acid which is, in part, responsible for their particular flavours. The structure of citric acid is to the right.

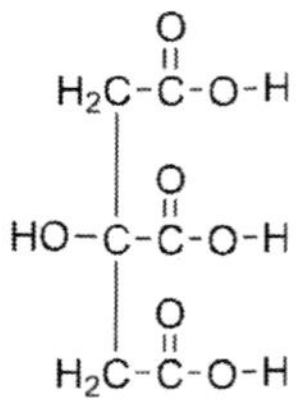

50. The functional groups within citric acid are

- **A.** ketones and alcohols
- **B.** aldehydes and carboxylic acids
- **C.** esters and alcohols
- **D.** alcohols and carboxylic acids

Use the following information to answer the next question.

Carvone is a compound whose molecules have **two structures** with the same formula ($C_{10}H_{14}O_2$) One geometric arrangement provides the characteristic odour of caraway seeds, while the other form gives the pleasant aroma of spearmint oil.

51. These two forms of carvone can best be described as

A. inorganic compounds
B. monomers
C. polymers
D. isomers

52. The third member of the homologous series of cycloalkanes (general formula C_nH_{2n}) is

A. C_3H_6
B. C_4H_8
C. C_5H_{10}
D. C_6H_{12}

Written Response

1. Define

a) atom

b) solution

c) mole

2. State Avogadro's Hypothesis.

3. What is the percent composition by mass of H_2CO_3?

4. Determine the molecular formula of a compound given its empirical formula is C_2H_6O and its molar mass is 138.0 g.

5. Consider the following reaction
$Fe_2O_3 + 3C \rightarrow 2Fe + 3CO$
What mass of Carbon is required to react completely with 100.0 g of the Iron III Oxide?

6. Magnesium has three naturally occurring isotopes: 23-Mg = 23.804 amu and has an abundance of 11.01%, 24-Mg = 23.985 amu and has an abundance of 79.99% and 25-Mg = 24.986 amu and has an abundance of 10.00%. Determine the atomic mass of Magnesium as it appears on the Periodic Table.

7. Showing all work, draw the electron (Lewis) dot diagram for

a) $CSCI_2$

b) PO_4^{-3}

8. Jacqueline dilutes the concentration of Chloride ions present in 125.0 mL of a 0.150 M NaCl solution by adding 75.0mL of 0.195M NaI. She has diluted the concentration of chloride ions but has she diluted the concentration of sodium ion? Show all work.

9. Draw the condensed structure for 4– ethyl – 3 – methyl – 2– heptene.

10. Name the compound.

Answers and Solutions – Practice Examination

1. B	12. C	23. D	34. A	45. B
2. A	13. D	24. A	35. B	46. C
3. D	14. B	25. D	36. C	47. A
4. A	15. D	26. B	37. A	48. B
5. C	16. A	27. C	38. C	49. A
6. D	17. A	28. A	39. A	50. D
7. A	18. A	29. A	40. D	51. D
8. A	19. C	30. A	41. A	52. C
9. A	20. C	31. D	42. A	
10. D	21. D	32. D	43. A	
11. A	22. A	33. A	44. D	

1. B

Litre is the base SI unit of volume and mL is variation on it.

2. A

There are 4 significant figures present in 56070 – the final zero is a place value and is not indicated to be significant as there is no decimal place present. The zero between the 6 and the 7 is significant.

3. D

In a multiplication or division involving significant figures the value with fewest sig figs is used to determine the number of sig figs in the answer. 6.02×10^{23} has 3 sig figs while 0.02457 has 4 so the answer will have 3.

4. A

To determine rate we would divide the mass by the time and end up with a rate in g/min or g/s. The latter is more correct as the SI unit of time is the second.

5. C

We know the point is between 16.2 and 16.4 and appears to be more than halfway between 16.2 and 16.4 so is at least 16.3. We cannot see how far past 16.3 the measure is as there is no marker so we can estimate and say halfway in this case thus 16.35. The five is a somewhat certain digit and is considered to have significance but us recognized as not precise.

6. D

All matter is considered to have mass and occupy volume.

7. A

All matter will have defining properties such as melting point, boiling point and density which can be used to identify it.

8. A

A chemical change alters the molecular composition of the matter which results in new substances which will have their own distinct properties.

9. A

An element consists of only one type of atom and therefore cannot be chemically reduced into any simpler substance. Compounds, solutions and polyatomic ions all consist of more than one type of atom and thus can be chemically altered into a simpler substance.

10. D

This is a metal – non-metal compound thus is an ionic compound. K is the symbol for Potassium which is always +1 and requires no roman numeral to indicate its charge. ClO_4^- is the Perchlorate ion and as no roman numerals are required the names are simply written together Potassium Perchlorate.

11. A

This again is an ionic compound. Mg is the symbol for Magnesium which always has a charge of +2 and thus does not require a roman numeral in the name to indicate its charge. PO_4^{-3} is the phosphate ion and as no roman numerals are required the names are simply written together Magnesium Phosphate.

12. C

This is a covalent compound as it is a composed of two non-metals. There is only a single Sulphur present so no prefix is required to indicate number of them. There are two chlorides present so a prefix, di, is required to indicate the number of chloride atoms in the compound – Sulphur dichloride.

13. D

Pb is Lead which does not have a consistent charge so a roman numeral is required to indicate its charge in the compound. O^{2-} is the oxide ion of which there are 2 in the compound. This gives us a total negative charge of 4 and as the sum of the charges in an ionic compound is zero there must be a positive charge of 4. There is only one Lead atom in the compound so it must have a charge of +4 – Lead IV Oxide.

14. B

This is an ionic compound despite NH_4^+ not being a metal – it is a positively charged polyatomic ion. Ammonium has a +1 charge while Oxalate has a -2 charge and as the charge sum of the compound equals zero we require two Ammonium ions to have a +2 to match the –2. There is a subscript 2 placed after the Ammonium to indicate that there are two of them present in the compound - $(NH_4)_2C_2O_4$.

15. D

This is a covalent compound as it is comprised of non-metals. The prefixes indicate the number of each atom present in the compound thus we would have two phosphorus atoms and five Chlorine atoms in the compound. The subscripts written indicate the number of atoms of each element that precedes them, P_2Cl_5.

16. A

The mole is the arbitrary unit used to relate the relative masses and quantities of atoms, molecules and ions to one another.

17. A

The molar mass of an element is equal to its atomic mass in grams. The atomic mass of Yttrium is 88.9 amu so its molar mass would be 88.9 g.

18. A

The molar mass is equal to the sum of the atomic masses of all the atoms present in the compound.

$$Mn(2\times 54.9g)+C(3\times 12.0g)+O(9\times 16.0g)$$
$$=289.8g$$

19. C

This is a unitary conversion form mass to moles.

$$32.0\,g\ CH_2O \times \frac{1\,mol}{30.0\,g\ CH_2O}$$

$$= 1.07\,mol\ CH_2O$$

20. C

Unitary conversion from moles to molecules

$$0.150\,mol\ RbCl \times \frac{6.02 \times 10^{23}\ molecules}{1\,mol}$$

$$= 9.03 \times 10^{22}\ molecules\ RbCl$$

21. D

Unitary conversion from mass to molecules. To do this we must first convert the mass to moles and then the moles can be converted to molecules

Plan: Mass KCl $\rightarrow$ moles KCl $\rightarrow$ molecules KCl

$$1.63 \times 10^{-3}\ g\ KCl \times \frac{1\,mol}{74.6\,g\ KCl} \times \frac{6.02 \times 10^{23}\ molecules}{1\,mol}$$

$$= 1.32 \times 10^{19}\ molecules\ KCl$$

22. A

Unitary conversion from moles of NO to Litres at STP

$$75.0\,mol\ NO \times \frac{22.4\,L}{1\,mol}$$

= 1680 L NO

23. D

This is a unitary conversion between mass and volume of a substance. Mass cannot directly be converted into volume and we must go through the unit mole. Any of the measures can be converted into moles and moles can be converted into any measure.

First change the volume into Litres

150.0mL = 0.1500L

Plan: L $Cl_2 \rightarrow$ mol $Cl_2 \rightarrow$ mass Cl_2

$$0.1500\,L\ Cl_2 \times \frac{1\,mol}{22.4\,L} \times \frac{32.0\,g}{1\,mol} = 0.4754\ g\ Cl_2$$

24. A

Step 1: Assume the mass of the compound analyzed to be 100.0g so that the percent by mass of the elements is easily determined: 57.45g C, 3.45g H and 39.1g F. Then follow the procedure for finding empirical formula: grams $\rightarrow$ mol: find ratio and ratio is empirical formula.

Step 2:

$$57.45\,g\ C \times \frac{1\,mol}{12.0\,g} = 4.788\,mol\,C$$

$$3.45\,g\ H \times \frac{1\,mol}{1.0\,g} = 3.45\,mol\,H$$

$$39.1\,g\ F \times \frac{1\,mol}{19.0\,g} = 2.05\,mol\,F$$

Step 3:

4.788 / 2.05 = 2.33 C

3.45 / 2.05 = 1.68 H

2.05 / 2.05 = 1 F

Step 4:

All ratios are multiplied by 3.

$C_{(2.33)\times 3}H_{(1.68)\times 3}F_{(1)\times 3}$

$C_7H_5F_3$

25. D

Molarity is a measure of concentration and is equal to the numbers of moles in a given volume M = mol/L. Molar concentration is another way of stating molarity.

26. B

Molarity = mol/L so to determine the molarity of the KI we simply divide the mol KI by the volume it is dissolving in.

$$\text{Molarity} = \frac{\text{mol}}{\text{L}} = \frac{0.350\,\text{mol}}{2.75\,\text{L}}$$
$$= 0.127\text{M KI}$$

27. C

We use the formula $\text{MV} = \frac{\text{mass}}{\text{g/mol}}$

$$(0.4500\text{M RbCl})(2.000\,\text{L}) = \frac{\text{mass RbCl}}{121.0\,\text{g/mol}}$$
$$\rightarrow \text{mass RbCl} = (0.4500)(2.000)(121.0)$$
$$\text{mass RbCl} = 108.9\text{ g}$$

28. A

When volumes are mixed the molarity of a solution will change. It changes because the molarity is volume dependent as it is a measure of the number of moles in a given volume. To determine the new molarity we us the dilution formula, $\text{M}_i\text{V}_i = \text{M}_f\text{V}_f$ where M is molarity, V is volume, i is initial and f is final. This basically finds the moles of the substance and divides it by the new volume.

$$\text{M}_i = 1.00\,\text{M} \quad \text{V}_i = 1.2500\,\text{L} \quad \text{M}_f = ?$$
$$\text{V}_f = 2.500\,\text{L} + 0.1500\,\text{L}$$
$$= 0.4000\,\text{L}$$
$$\text{M}_i = \frac{(1.00\,\text{M})(0.2500\,\text{L})}{(0.4000\,\text{L})}$$
$$= 0.625\text{ M } HNO_3$$

29. A

The reaction is in a closed system meaning nothing is entering or leaving the reaction vessel. It involves no gases being consumed or produced so the mass of the reaction vessel and its contents can be taken before and after the reaction accurately. We cannot measure the mass of a gas directly. A chemical reaction involves the reactant atoms rearranging to form the products so the mass of the reactants should, given the Law of Conservation of Mass, equal the mass of the products.

30. A

This reaction is a combustion reaction. They can be identified by a Hydrocarbon compound reacting with Oxygen to form Carbon Dioxide and Water. These components are always present in a combustion reaction even though it may contain other substances as well.

31. D

This is a double replacement reaction. They can be recognized as the reactants are both ionic compounds and the products are formed by the metals of the reactants switching places with the respective non-metals. Note in the above reaction that the Ag^+ is originally with the NO_3^- as a reactant and finishes with the Cl^- as a product while the Na^+ starts with the Cl^- as a reactant and finishes with the NO_3^- as a product.

32. D

This reaction is a decomposition and they are easily recognizable as they have only one reactant compound which forms two or more products.

33. A

A balanced chemical reaction is necessary to reflect the Law of Conservation of Mass. Given that the reactants are rearranging to form the products there must be the same number of atoms of each element on the reactant side of the reaction as there is on the product side of the reaction. This of course is the reason that the mass of the products will equal the mass of the reactants as per the Law of conservation of Mass. We can only use coefficients to change the numbers of atoms of the elements as changing any of the subscripts will change what the actual substance is.

34. A

Firstly this is a synthesis and/or combination reaction. These reaction types can be recognized by there being two lone elements as the reactants, H_2 and Cl_2 in this reaction, which combine to form a single compound as the product, HCl. The change in enthalpy for this reaction is –185kJ. It is a negative value because it appears as a product indicating the products have less enthalpy, potential energy, than the reactants. When energy is lost in the system it has been released into the environment and the reaction is called Exothermic.

35. B

We can determine the moles of O_2 required directly as it is possible to do calculations within a balanced chemical reaction as long as you have the unit mole.

$$6.0\,\text{mol NO} \times \frac{5\,\text{mol O}_2}{4\,\text{mol NO}}$$

$$= 7.5\ \text{mol O}_2$$

36. C

The limiting reagent is the reactant that is consumed first and thus stops the reaction and limits the amount of the product that can be produced. We can use molar ratio numbers to see how many moles of $AgNO_3$ are required to react with the Cu in the question.

First we need to find moles of each reactant

$$16.0\,\text{g Cu} \times \frac{1\,\text{mol}}{63.5\,\text{g Cu}} = 0.252\text{mol Cu } 42.0\,\text{g}$$

$$\text{AgNO}_3 \times \frac{1\,\text{mol}}{169.9\,\text{g AgNO}_3} = 0.247\ \text{mol}$$

$$\text{AgNO}_3$$

$$\frac{\text{Cu}}{0.252\,\text{mol}} = \frac{2\,\text{AgNO}_3}{x}$$

x = the moles $AgNO_3$ required to react with 0.252mol Cu

$x = 0.504$mol $AgNO_3$ as we only have 0.247 mol $AgNO_3$ it is the limiting reagent.

37. A

The neutrons and the protons make up the mass of the atom and have essentially the same mass equal to one. Therefore the mass of the atom minis the number (thus mass) of the protons will equal the number (and mass) of the neutrons. Recall number of protons is equivalent to the atomic number.

Number neutrons = atomic mass – atomic number

Number neutrons = 144.2 – 60

= 84.2 = 84 neutrons

38. C

The number of protons in the nucleus of any element's atom is equivalent to the element's atomic number. The atomic number of Iridium is 77 therefore it has 77 protons in the nucleus.

39. A

P^{3-} is an ion with a –3 charge. This indicates there are three more electrons present than protons, electrons having a negative charge and protons having a positive charge. The number of protons never changes; therefore, the atom has gained and electron and the total will be the number of protons (atomic number) plus three.

Number electrons = atomic number + 3

= 15 + 3 = 18 electrons

40. D

Ti is a neutral atom therefore the number of electrons is equal to the number of protons. The number of protons is equivalent to the atomic number which is 22. The electrons are placed into the orbits and sub shells filling the lowest energy levels first: Order of electron filling:

$1s \rightarrow 2s \rightarrow 2p \rightarrow 3s \rightarrow 3p \rightarrow 4s \rightarrow 3d \rightarrow 4p \rightarrow 5s \rightarrow 4d \rightarrow 5p \rightarrow 6s \rightarrow 4f \ldots$

remembering that s holds 2 electrons, p holds 6 electrons, d holds 10 electrons and f holds 14 electrons.

41. A

Mn+4 is an ion therefore the number of electrons is not equal to the number of protons. The number of protons is equivalent to the atomic number which is 25 for Manganese. The +4 charge means there is 4 more protons present than electrons indicating the atom has lost 4 electrons. The number of electrons is then 25 – 4 = 21. The electrons are placed into the orbits and sub shells filling the lowest energy levels first: Order of electron filling:

$1s \rightarrow 2s \rightarrow 2p \rightarrow 3s \rightarrow 3p \rightarrow 4s \rightarrow 3d \rightarrow 4p \rightarrow 5s \rightarrow 4d \rightarrow 5p \rightarrow 6s \rightarrow 4f \ldots$

remembering that s holds 2 electrons, p holds 6 electrons, d holds 10 electrons and f holds 14 electrons.

42. A

Column 14 elements are in the P – block and thus the final valance electrons are in the p subshell. Column 14 is the second column in the p block and all elements in this column have 2 electrons in the p subshell while in ground state.

43. A

The alkaline earth metals are those elements in column 2 of the periodic table and Sr is in column (group) 2.

44. D

Halogens are non-metals and do not have any metallic properties. The properties in b,c and d are all those of metals while diatomic in the gaseous phase is a specific property of the halogens.

45. B

The elements in column 15 end in s^2p^3 and require 3 more electrons to have the electronic configuration of the noble gases which is full valence, s^2p^6.

46. C

When there is an electronegativity difference between the substances of between 0.2 and 1.7 there will be a partial electron transfer from the substance with the lower electronegativity to the substance with the higher electronegativity. This results with a substance having a partial positive charge and a substance with a partial negative charge. The partially charged atoms are called dipoles.

47. A

Phosphorus and chlorine are both non-metals so this will not be an ionic bond. We do not have the electronegativities of the elements so it is not possible to determine the exact nature of the bond, polar covalent versus covalent therefore the best answer is a covalent bond.

48. B

Chlorine is a molecular element held together by a single covalent bond. Since each bonded atom has the same electronegativity, the electrons are shared equally.

49. A

Only molecules that contain polar bonds can be polar and then only if the bond dipoles do not cancel as a consequence of molecular geometry. Thus the V.S.E.P.R. shape of a molecule is necessary to predict that molecule's polarity.

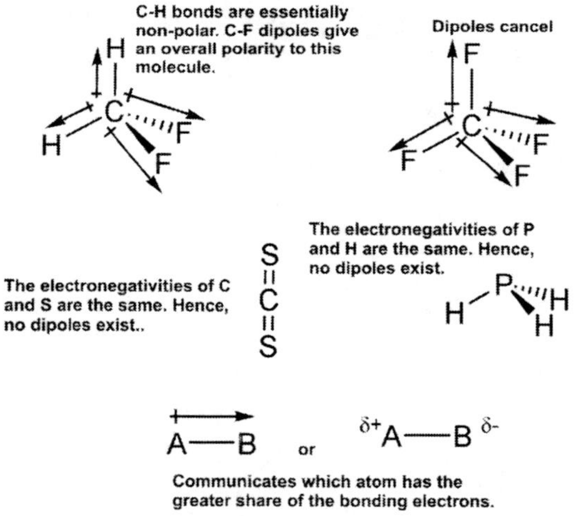

50. D

The structural feature of an organic molecule that allows us to classify that molecule by its reactivity is called a functional group.

Some important functional groups are shown in the adjacent column.

The important functional groups in citric acid are those of alcohols and carboxylic acids.

51. D

Isomers are compounds that have the same chemical formula but different chemical structures. More often than not isomers have different chemical and/or physical properties. Without knowing the precise structures of carvone (other than that it is an organic compound), its two forms meet the qualification for isomers.

52. C

The first cycloalkene is cyclopropane, C_3H_6, the second is cyclobutane, C_4H_8, and the third member is cyclopentane, C_5H_{10}. These are shown below.

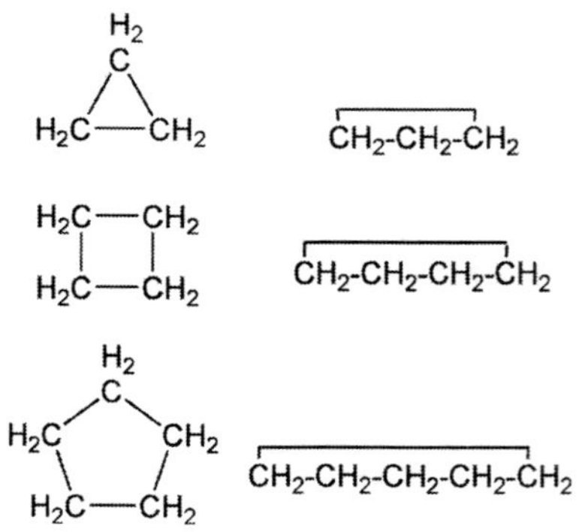

Written Response

1. Define **a)** atom – the smallest possible unit of an element possible which will still retain the properties of the element.

b) solution – a homogenous mixture containing 2 or more substances.

c) mole – the mole is the number of particles of Carbon in 12 grams of C-12. The atomic masses of all other elements are relative to that of C-12 so one mole of any element contains the same numbers of particle as one mole of
C-12.

2. State Avogadro's Hypothesis – Equal volumes of different gases, at the same temperature and pressure, contain the same number of particles.

3. What is the percent composition by mass of H_2CO_3?

To determine the percent composition by mass of all the elements in the compound, H_2CO_3, we must divide the sum of the masses for each element by the molar mass of the compound and multiply by 100.
Mass H = 2 × 1.0 = 2.0 g
Mass C = 1 × 12.0 = 12.0 g
Mass O = 3 × 16.0 = 48.0 g
Molar mass H_2CO_3 = 2.0 g
H + 12.0 g
C + 48.0 g
O = 62.0 g H_2CO_3
% by mass H = (2.0g/62.0g) × 100
H = 3.2%
% by mass Mn = (12.0g/62.0g) × 100
C = 19.4%
% by mass O = (48.0g/62.0g) × 100
O = 77.4%

4. Determine the molecular formula of a compound given its empirical formula is C_2H_6O and its molar mass is 138.0 g
$(C_2H_6O)_n$ = 138.0 g therefore
$(46.0g)_n$ = 138.0 g and n = 138.0/46.0 = 3
So $(C_2H_6O)_3 = C_6H_{18}O_3$

5. Consider the following reaction:
$Fe_2O_3 + 3C \rightarrow 2Fe + 3CO$
What mass of Carbon is required to react completely with 100.0g of the Iron III Oxide?

Plan: Mass
$Fe_2O_3 \rightarrow$ moles $Fe_2O_3 \rightarrow$ moles $C \rightarrow$ mass C

$$100.0\,g\ Fe_2O_3 \times \frac{1\,mol}{159.6\,g\ Fe_2O_3} \times \frac{3\,mol\,C}{1\,mol\ Fe_2O_3} \times \frac{12.0\,g\,C}{1\,mol}$$

= 22.56 g C

6. Magnesium has three naturally occurring isotopes: 23-Mg = 23.804amu and has an abundance of 11.01%, 24-Mg = 23.985amu and has an abundance of 79.99% and 25-Mg = 24.986amu and has an abundance of 10.00%. Determine the atomic mass of Magnesium as it appears on the periodic table.

The atomic mass as it appears on the periodic table is a relative average of the isotopes of the element.
Atomic mass = (fraction of isotope) (mass of isotope) + (fraction of isotope)(mass of isotope) + …
Atomic mass = (0.1101 × 23.804) + (0.7999 × 23.985) + (0.1000 × 24.986)
= 24.305 amu

7. **Showing all work draw the electron (Lewis) dot diagram for**

a) $CsCl_2$

$CSCl_2$

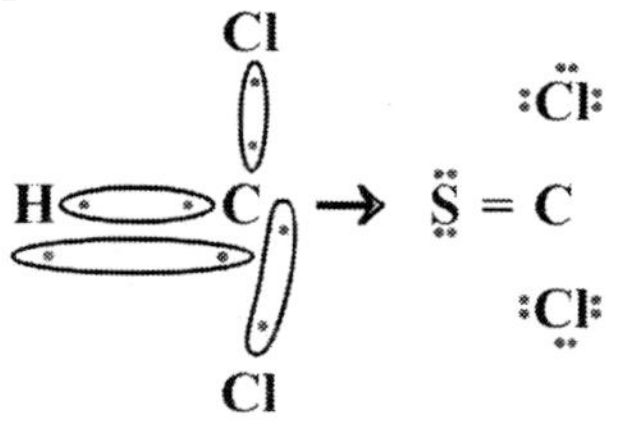

b) PO_4^{3-}

PO_4^{3-}

$5 + 4 \times 6 + 3 = 32$

P O

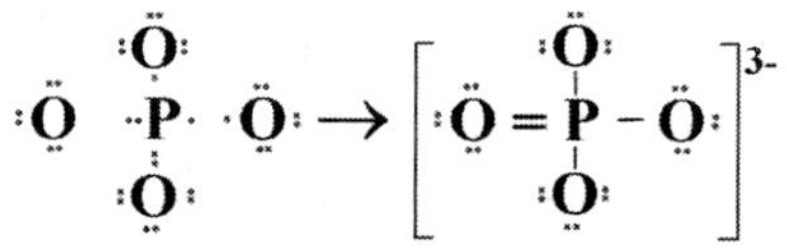

8. Jacqueline dilutes the concentration of Chloride ions present in 125.0mL of a 0.150M NaCl solution by adding 75.0mL of 0.195M NaI. She has diluted the concentration of chloride ions but has she diluted the concentration of sodium ion? Show all work.

First calculate the molarities of the compounds after the dilution using the dilution formula $M_iV_i = M_fV_f$

$$\text{Diluted [NaCl]} = \frac{(0.150\,\text{M})(0.1250\,\text{L})}{(0.2000\,\text{L})}$$
$$= 0.0938\ \text{M NaCl}$$

$$\text{Diluted [NaI]} = \frac{(0.195\,\text{M})(0.0750\,\text{L})}{(0.2000\,\text{L})}$$
$$= 0.0731\ \text{M NaI}$$

Secondly write the dissociation equations for the compounds and from them determine the concentration of the ions.

$$NaCl_{(s)} \rightarrow Na^+_{(aq)} + Cl^-_{(aq)}$$
0.0938M so 0.938M 0.0938M

$$NaI_{(s)} \rightarrow Na^+_{(aq)} + I^-_{(aq)}$$
0.0731M so 0.0731M 0.0731M

$[Na^+] = 0.0938 + 0.0731 = 0.167M$
Concentration of Na+ went up to 0.167M from 0.150M in the original solution.

9. Draw the condensed structure for 4 – ethyl – 3 – methyl – 2 – heptene.

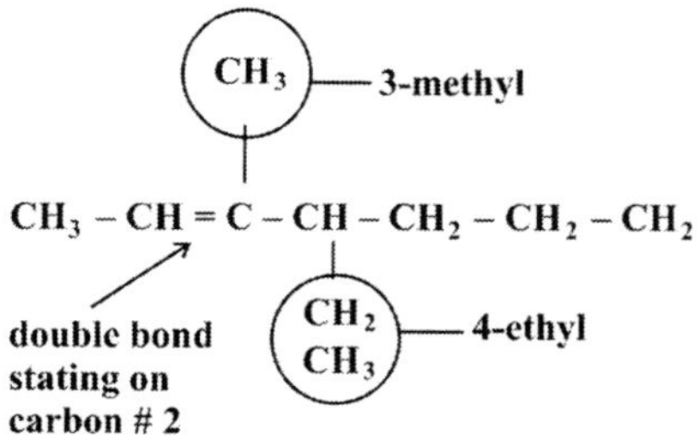

10. Name the compound.

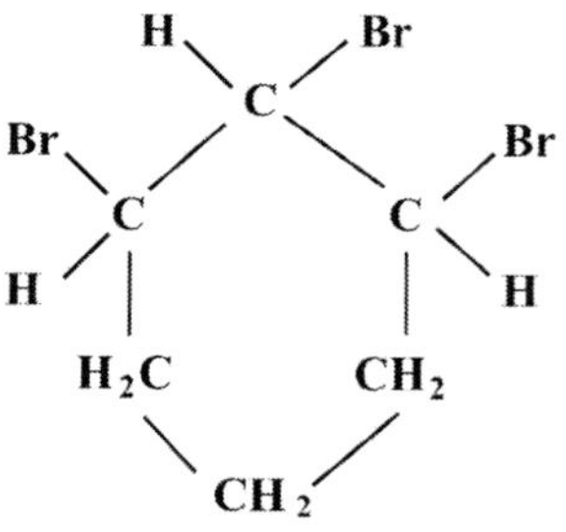

= 1, 3 – dibromo – 2 – methyl – cyclohexane

Data Booklet

Chemistry 11—Data Sheets

Common Formulas and Units of Measurement

- *STP conditions:* 0° C (273.15 K) and 1 atm (101.325 kPa) pressure.
- *SATP conditions:* 25°C (298.15 K) and 100 kPa pressure.
- *Molar Volumes:* V_{STP} = 22.4 L and V_{SATP} = 24.8 L
- 1 atm = 101.325 kPa = 760 mm Hg = 760 torr
- T(K)= T (°C) + 273.15
- *Ideal Gas Law:* $PV = nRT$
- *Combined Gas Law:* $\frac{P_1V_1}{T_1} = \frac{P_2V_2}{T_2}$
- *The Gas Constant:* $R = 8.314 \frac{\text{L} \cdot \text{kPa}}{\text{mol} \cdot \text{K}}$ or $0.08206 \frac{\text{L} \cdot \text{atm}}{\text{mol} \cdot \text{K}}$
- *Avogadro's Number:* $N_A = 6.022 \times 10^{23}$
- $K_w = 1.0 \times 10^{-14} \left(\frac{mol}{L}\right)^2$ at 25°C
- pH = –log $[H^+_{(aq)}]$ *note:* ($[H^+_{(aq)}]$ in $\frac{\text{moL}}{\text{L}}$)
- $[H^+_{(aq)}] = 10^{-\text{pH}}$
- $C_1V_1 = C_2V_2$ (for dilution only)

SOLUBILITY OF SOME COMMON IONIC COMPOUNDS IN WATER AT 298.15 K (25°C)

ION	Group IA NH_4^+ $H^+(H_3O^+)$	ClO_3^- NO_3^- ClO_4^-	CH_3COO^-	Cl^- Br^- I^-	SO_4^{2-}	S^{2-}	OH^-	PO_4^{3-} SO_3^{2-} CO_3^{2-}
Solubility greater than or equal to 0.1 mol/L (very soluble)	all	all	most	most	most	Group IA Group IIA NH_4^+	Group IA NH_4^+ Sr^{2+} Ba^{2+} Tl^+	Group IA NH_4^+
Solubility less than 0.1 mol/L (slightly soluble)	none	none	Ag^+ Hg^+	Ag^+ Pb^{2+} Hg^+ Cu^+ Tl^+	Ca^{2+} Sr^{2+} Ba^{2+} Ra^{2+} Pb^{2+} Ag^+	most	most	most

COLOR CHART OF COMMON AQUEOUS IONS

ION	SYMBOL	COLOR
chromate	CrO_4^{2-}	yellow
chromium(III)	Cr^{3+}	green
chromium(II)	Cr^{2+}	blue
cobalt(II)	Co^{2+}	pink
copper(I)	Cu^+	green
copper(II)	Cu^{2+}	blue
dichromate	$Cr_2O_7^{2-}$	orange
iron(II)	Fe^{2+}	pale green
iron(III)	Fe^{3+}	pale yellow
manganese(II)	Mn^{2+}	pale pink
permanganate	MnO_4^-	purple

PERIODIC CHART OF THE ELEMENTS

1	2	3	4	5	6	7	8	9	10	11	12	13	14	15	16	17	18
IA	IIA	IIIB	IVB	VB	VIB	VIIB		VIIIB		IB	IIB	IIIA	IVA	VA	VIA	VIIA	VIIIA or O
1 H 2.1 hydrogen 1.01																	2 He – helium 4.00
3 Li 1.0 lithium 6.94	4 Be 1.5 beryllium 9.01											5 B 2.0 boron 10.81	6 C 2.5 carbon 12.01	7 N 3.0 nitrogen 14.01	8 O 3.5 oxygen 16.00	9 F 4.0 fluorine 19.00	10 Ne – neon 20.17
11 Na 0.9 sodium 22.99	12 Mg 1.2 magnesium 24.31											13 Al 1.5 aluminum 26.98	14 Si 1.8 silicon 28.09	15 P 2.1 phosphorus 30.97	16 S 2.5 sulphur 32.06	17 Cl 3.0 chlorine 35.45	18 Ar – argon 39.95
19 K 0.8 potassium 39.10	20 Ca 1.0 calcium 40.08	21 Sc 1.3 scandium 44.96	22 Ti 1.5 titanium 47.90	23 V 1.6 vanadium 50.94	24 Cr 1.6 chromium 52.00	25 Mn 1.5 manganese 54.94	26 Fe 1.8 iron 55.85	27 Co 1.8 cobalt 58.93	28 Ni 1.8 nickel 58.71	29 Cu 1.9 copper 63.55	30 Zn 1.6 zinc 65.38	31 Ga 1.6 gallium 69.74	32 Ge 1.8 germanium 72.59	33 As 2.0 arsenic 74.92	34 Se 2.4 selenium 78.96	35 Br 2.8 bromine 79.90	36 Kr – krypton 83.80
37 Rb 0.8 rubidium 85.47	38 Sr 1.0 strontium 87.62	39 Y 1.3 yttrium 88.91	40 Zr 1.4 zirconium 91.22	41 Nb 1.6 niobium 92.91	42 Mo 1.8 molybdenum 95.94	43 Tc 1.9 technetium 98.91	44 Ru 2.2 ruthenium 101.07	45 Rh 2.2 rhodium 102.91	46 Pd 2.2 palladium 106.40	47 Ag 1.9 silver 107.87	48 Cd 1.7 cadmium 112.41	49 In 1.7 indium 114.82	50 Sn 1.8 tin 118.69	51 Sb 1.9 antimony 121.75	52 Te 2.1 tellurium 127.60	53 I 2.5 iodine 126.90	54 Xe – xenon 131.30
55 Cs 0.7 cesium 132.91	56 Ba 0.9 barium 137.33	57-71	72 Hf 1.3 hafnium 178.49	73 Ta 1.5 tantalum 180.95	74 W 1.7 tungsten 183.85	75 Re 1.9 rhenium 186.21	76 Os 2.2 osmium 190.20	77 Ir 2.2 iridium 192.22	78 Pt 2.2 platinum 195.09	79 Au 2.4 gold 196.97	80 Hg 1.9 mercury 200.59	81 Tl 1.8 thallium 204.37	82 Pb 1.8 lead 207.19	83 Bi 1.9 bismuth 208.98	84 Po 2.0 polonium (209)	85 At 2.2 astatine (210)	86 Rn – radon (222)
87 Fr 0.7 francium (223)	88 Ra 0.9 radium 226.03	89-103	104 Unq – unnilquadium (260)	105 Unp – unnilpentium (260)	106 Unh – unnihexium (263)	107 Uns – unnilseptium (262)	108 Uno – unniloctium (265)	109 Une – unnilennium (266)									

KEY

ATOMIC NUMBER →	1
ELECTRONEGATIVITY →	2.1
NAME OF THE ELEMENT →	hydrogen
ATOMIC MASS →	1.01
H ← SYMBOL OF THE ELEMENT	

BASED ON $^{12}_{6}C$

( ) INDICATES MASS OF THE MOST STABLE ISOTOPE

NOTE: The legend at right denotes the physical state of the elements at 101 kPa and 298.15 K (25°C)

LEGEND

SOLID

LIQUID

GAS

57 La 1.1 lanthanum 138.91	58 Ce 1.1 cerium 140.12	59 Pr 1.1 praseodynium 140.91	60 Nd 1.2 neodymium 144.24	61 Pm – promethium (145)	62 Sm 1.2 samarium 150.35	63 Eu – europium 151.96	64 Gd 1.1 gadolinium 157.25	65 Tb 1.2 terbium 158.93	66 Dy – dysprosium 162.50	67 Ho 1.2 holmium 164.93	68 Er 1.2 erbium 167.26	69 Tm 1.2 thulium 168.93	70 Yb 1.1 ytterbium 173.04	71 Lu 1.2 lutetium 174.97
89 Ac 1.1 actinium (227)	90 Th 1.3 thorium 232.04	91 Pa 1.5 protactinium 231.04	92 U 1.7 uranium 238.03	93 Np 1.3 neptunium 237.05	94 Pu 1.3 plutonium (244)	95 Am 1.3 americium (243)	96 Cm – curium (247)	97 Bk – berkelium (247)	98 Cf – californium (251)	99 Es – einsteinium (254)	100 Fm – fermium (257)	101 Md – mendelevium (258)	102 No – nobelium (259)	103 Lr – lawrencium (260)

PERIODIC CHART OF IONS

TABLE OF POLYATOMIC IONS

acetate	CH_3COO^-	dichromate	$Cr_2O_7^{2-}$	dihydrogen phosphate	$H_2PO_4^-$
ammonium	NH_4^+	cyanide	CN^-	silicate	SiO_3^{2-}
benzoate	$C_6H_5COO^-$	hydroxide	OH^-	sulphate	SO_4^{2-}
borate	BO_3^{3-}	iodate	IO_3^-	sulphite	SO_3^{2-}
carbonate	CO_3^{2-}	nitrate	NO_3^-	hydrogen sulphide	HS^-
hydrogen carbonate	HCO_3^-	nitrite	NO_2^-	hydrogen sulphate	HSO_4^-
chlorate	ClO_3^-	oxalate	$OOCCOO^{2-}$	hydrogen sulphite	HSO_3^-
hypochlorite	ClO^-	permanganate	MnO_4^-	thiocyanate	SCN^-
chromate	CrO_4^{2-}	phosphate	PO_4^{3-}	thiosulphate	$S_2O_3^{2-}$
		hydrogen phosphate	HPO_4^{2-}		

1 H^+ hydrogen																1 H^- hydride	2 **He** helium
3 Li^+ lithium	4 Be^{2+} beryllium											5 **B** boron	6 **C** carbon	7 N^{3-} nitride	8 O^{2-} oxide	9 F^- fluoride	10 **Ne** neon
11 Na^+ sodium	12 Mg^{2+} magnesium											13 Al^{3+} aluminum	14 **Si** silicon	15 P^{3-} phosphide	16 S^{2-} sulphide	17 Cl^- chloride	18 **Ar** argon
19 K^+ potassium	20 Ca^{2+} calcium	21 Sc^{3+} scandium	22 Ti^{4+} titanium(IV) / Ti^{3+} titanium(III)	23 V^{5+} vanadium(V) / V^{4+} vanadium(IV)	24 Cr^{3+} chromium(III) / Cr^{2+} chromium(II)	25 Mn^{2+} manganese(II) / Mn^{4+} manganese(IV)	26 Fe^{3+} iron(III) / Fe^{2+} iron(II)	27 Co^{2+} cobalt(II) / Co^{3+} cobalt(III)	28 Ni^{2+} nickel(II) / Ni^{3+} nickel(III)	29 Cu^{2+} copper(II) / Cu^+ copper(I)	30 Zn^{2+} zinc	31 Ga^{3+} gallium	32 Ge^{4+} germanium	33 As^{3-} arsenide	34 Se^{2-} selenide	35 Br^- bromide	36 **Kr** krypton
37 Rb^+ rubidium	38 Sr^{2+} strontium	39 Y^{3+} yttrium	40 Zr^{4+} zirconium	41 Nb^{5+} niobium(V) / Nb^{3+} niobium(III)	42 Mo^{6+} molybdenum	43 Tc^{7+} technetium	44 Ru^{3+} ruthenium(III) / Ru^{4+} ruthenium(IV)	45 Rh^{3+} rhodium	46 Pd^{2+} palladium(II) / Pd^{4+} palladium(IV)	47 Ag^+ silver	48 Cd^{2+} cadmium	49 In^{3+} indium	50 Sn^{4+} tin(IV) / Sn^{2+} tin(II)	51 Sb^{3+} antimony(III) / Sb^{5+} antimony(V)	52 Te^{2-} telluride	53 I^- iodide	54 **Xe** xenon
55 Cs^+ cesium	56 Ba^{2+} barium	57-71	72 Hf^{4+} hafnium	73 Ta^{5+} tantalum	74 W^{6+} tungsten	75 Re^{7+} rhenium	76 Os^{4+} osmium	77 Ir^{4+} iridium	78 Pt^{4+} platinum(IV) / Pt^{2+} platinum(II)	79 Au^{3+} gold(III) / Au^+ gold(I)	80 Hg^{2+} mercury(II) / Hg^+ mercury(I)	81 Tl^+ thallium(I) / Tl^{3+} thallium(III)	82 Pb^{2+} lead(II) / Pb^{4+} lead(IV)	83 Bi^{3+} bismuth(III) / Bi^{5+} bismuth(V)	84 Po^{2+} polonium(II) / Po^{4+} polonium(IV)	85 At astatide	86 **Rn** radon
87 Fr^+ francium	88 Ra^{2+} radium	89-103															

KEY

atomic number → 26 Fe^{3+} ← ion charge
iron(III) ← stock name (IUPAC)
Fe^{2+} ← symbol
iron(II)

57 La^{3+} lanthanum	58 Ce^{3+} cerium	59 Pr^{3+} praseodymium	60 Nd^{3+} neodymium	61 Pm^{3+} promethium	62 Sm^{3+} samarium(III) / Sm^{2+} samarium(II)	63 Eu^{3+} europium(III) / Eu^{2+} europium(II)	64 Gd^{3+} gadolinium	65 Tb^{3+} terbium	66 Dy^{3+} dysprosium	67 Ho^{3+} holmium	68 Er^{3+} erbium	69 Tm^{3+} thulium	70 Yb^{3+} ytterbium(III) / Yb^{2+} ytterbium(II)	71 Lu^{3+} lutetium
89 Ac^{3+} actinium	90 Th^{4+} thorium	91 Pa^{5+} protactinium(V) / Pa^{4+} protactinium(IV)	92 U^{6+} uranium(VI) / U^{4+} uranium(IV)	93 Np^{5+} neptunium	94 Pu^{4+} plutonium(IV) / Pu^{6+} plutonium(VI)	95 Am^{3+} americium(III) / Am^{4+} americium(IV)	96 Cm^{3+} curium	97 Bk^{3+} berkelium(III) / Bk^{4+} berkelium(IV)	98 Cf^{3+} californium	99 Es^{3+} einsteinium	100 Fm^{3+} fermium	101 Md^{2+} mendelevium(II) / Md^{3+} mendelevium(III)	102 No^{2+} nobelium(II) / No^{3+} nobelium(III)	103 Lr^{3+} lawrencium

Credits

ORDERING INFORMATION

INDIVIDUAL ORDERS	SCHOOL ORDERS
ORDER ONLINE at **www.castlerockresearch.com** or contact Castle Rock Research BC Toll-free: 1.866.882.8246 Fax: 250.868.9146	Schools and school jurisdictions are eligible for our **educational discount** rate. Contact Castle Rock Research BC for more information.

***THE KEY** Study Guides* are specifically designed to assist students in preparing for unit tests, final exams, and provincial examinations.

***KEY** Study Guides* – $29.95 each plus G.S.T.

SENIOR HIGH		JUNIOR HIGH	ELEMENTARY
Biology 12 Chemistry 12 English 12 Geography 12 History 12 Physics 12 Principles of Math 12	Biology 11 Chemistry 11 English 11 Physics 11 Principles of Math 11 English 10 Principles of Math 10 Science 10	Language Arts 9 Math 9 Language Arts 7 Math 7	Math 6 Language Arts 4 Math 4

Student Notes and Problems (SNAP) Workbooks contain complete explanations of curriculum concepts, examples, and exercise questions.

SNAP Workbooks – $29.95 each plus G.S.T.

SENIOR HIGH		JUNIOR HIGH	ELEMENTARY
Principles of Math 12 Physics 12	Principles of Math 11 Physics 11 Principles of Math 10	Science 9 Math 9 Math 8 Math 7	Math 6 Math 5 Math 4 Math 3

For students in the following courses, we have available the following corresponding resources which are correlated to the B.C. curriculum.

B.C. COURSE NAME	CORRESPONDING RESOURCE
Applications of Math 12	***THE KEY*** – Math 30 Applied
Applications of Math 12	**SNAP** – Math 30 Applied
Applications of Math 11	**SNAP** – Math 20 Applied
Applications of Math 10	**SNAP** – Math 10 Applied
Calculus 12	**SNAP** – Math 31

Visit our website for a "tour" of resource content and features, or order online at

www.castlerockresearch.com

ORDER FORM

ORDER ONLINE AT www.castlerockresearch.com

THE KEY	Price	Quantity	Total
Biology 12	$29.95		
Chemistry 12	$29.95		
English 12	$29.95		
Geography 12	$29.95		
History 12	$29.95		
Physics 12	$29.95		
Principles of Math 12	$29.95		
Biology 11	$29.95		
Chemistry 11	$29.95		
English 11	$29.95		
Physics 11	$29.95		
Principles of Math 11	$29.95		
English 10	$29.95		
Principles of Math 10	$29.95		
Science 10	$29.95		
Language Arts 9	$29.95		
Math 9	$29.95		
Language Arts 7	$29.95		
Math 7	$29.95		
Math 6	$29.95		
Language Arts 4	$29.95		
Math 4	$29.95		

SUBTOTAL 1

SNAP WORKBOOKS	Price	Quantity	Total
Physics 12	$29.95		
Principles of Math 12	$29.95		
Physics 11	$29.95		
Principles of Math 11	$29.95		
Principles of Math 10	$29.95		
Science 9	$29.95		
Math 9	$29.95		
Math 8	$29.95		
Math 7	$29.95		
Math 6	$29.95		
Math 5	$29.95		
Math 4	$29.95		
Math 3	$29.95		

SUBTOTAL 2

TOTAL COST OF BOOKS

SUBTOTAL 1	
SUBTOTAL 2	
SUBTOTAL 3	
COST SUBTOTAL	
SHIPPING AND HANDLING Please call for current rates	
G.S.T.	
ORDER TOTAL	

For students in the following courses, we recommend the corresponding Alberta resources which are highly correlated to the B.C. curriculum.

B.C. Course Name	Alberta Resource	Price	Quantity	Total
Applications of Math 12	THE KEY - Math 30 Applied	$29.95		
Applications of Math 12	SNAP - Math 30 Applied	$29.95		
Applications of Math 11	SNAP - Math 20 Applied	$29.95		
Applications of Math 10	SNAP - Math 10 Applied	$29.95		
Calculus 12	SNAP - Math 31	$29.95		

SUBTOTAL 3

Significant discounts for school orders. Prices subject to change.

Please complete the shipping and payment information.

Name: ____________________

Mailing Address: ____________________

City: ____________________ Postal Code: ____________________

Telephone: ____________________ School: ____________________

VISA/MC Card Number: ____________________ Expiry Date (mm/yy): ____________________

Name on Card: ____________________

ORDERING OPTIONS

On-line: www.castlerockresearch.com

Telephone: 250.868.8384 or 866.882.8246

Fax: 250.868.9146

E-mail: learnbc@castlerockresearch.com

Mail: #4 - 1905 Evergreen Court, Kelowna, BC V1Y 9L4

OR CONTACT YOUR DISTRICT REPRESENTATIVE

(Visit our website for the name of the representative in your area.)

Castle Rock Research BC

www.castlerockresearch.com